Intercultural
Communication

Intercultural Communication

L. E. Sarbaugh

Revised, with a new Preface by the Author

Transaction Books
New Brunswick (USA) and Oxford (UK)

Library of Congress Catalog Number: 87-25578
ISBN 0-88738-719-5
Printed in the United States of America

Library of Congress Cataloging in Publication Data

Sarbaugh, L. E.
  Intercultural communication.

  Bibliography: p.
  Includes index.
  1. Intercultural communication. 2. Communication—
Social aspects. I. Title.
HM258.S262   1987   303.4'82   87-25578
ISBN 0-88738-719-5

Preface to the Transaction Edition

This edition adds a bit to the material in the first edition, building on what is believed to be a meaningful framework for conceptualizing the levels of interculturalness among those who seek to communicate.

In this preface, I will call attention to some intercultural experiences I have had since retiring three years ago, and some work that has been done with world view scales and the search for people typologies. Both of those sets of experiences confirm for me the usefulness of thinking about intercultural communication in terms of some kind of taxonomy based on a continuum of homogeneity–heterogeneity of participants.

One need only look at the types of conflicts and the ways of dealing with them in our own communities, state, nation, and among various peoples of the world to see how urgent it is that we seek to improve the ways we relate to one another, and our communication knowledge and skills are central to that task. The communication settings range from conflicts within families to those involving nations. From settings in which consensus is reached amicably to those in which physical violence erupts. Between spouses and among parents and children; between labor and management; on issues of international trade, war and peace, and environmental management for the well being of generations yet unborn.

Too often, we have persons from different countries in official positions who attempt to communicate on critical issues affecting both countries without adequate skills in the code systems or values and beliefs of the other society. Not only do their decisions and actions affect their own countries, but frequently many other countries of the world as well.

U.S. assets in other countries of the world have increased from about $55 billion in 1950, to nearly $915 billion in 1984. On the other hand, assets of other countries of the world invested in the U.S. have increased from about $18 billion in 1950 to more than $885 billion in 1984. (Data are from U.S. Statistical Abstracts, 1986 edition.) I cite these data as an indicator of the increasing levels of activity and interaction among foreign nationals to carry on business in the world, and the implied urgency of improving communication among people of the world.

In the three years since retirement, I have been working on the issue of poverty in a small rural community, and volunteering in the local elementary school. This has been an enlightening experience in many ways and has called attention to some intercultural communication situations in our local communities.

One of the women on welfare stated the intercultural communication problem for me in this local setting quite well when she said,

> Perhaps I shouldn't say this, but it's true; so, I'll say it. People in my situation think people like you don't understand what life is like for us and you have difficulty talking with us about it.

This and similar experiences have highlighted for me the validity of the claim that there is much to experience and learn about intercultural communication within our own communities.

Another example within the local community occurred this week as I was writing this copy. A lad, nearly 16, soon to enter the labor market, insisted the time that elapsed between 4:30 p.m. and 6 p.m. was two and a half hours. Drawing a circle with clock hands was not much help for someone who had only seen digital clocks and whose math skills were limited. Six stalks of grass broken in half was of some help in pointing out that one and a half stalks (hours) remained after four and a half had been removed to establish the starting time (4:30). This highlighted for me once again the difficulties of communicating with someone who operates on a different level of code and conceptual skills.

Another lad who wants to learn to read and to get his drivers' license this year, cannot read the words that appear on traffic signs. Some may say these cases are unusual, but I have come to believe that many cases of miscommunication occur within our societies and between societies, and go unidentified, or are simply ignored because it would take too much energy to deal with them.

In the county in which I now live, the literacy council lists 11,000 of the 55,000 adults as functionally nonliterate. The definition for nonliterate is that the person could not read a menu in a restaurant to order a meal, could not use a telephone directory, could not use a checkbook, or read a newspaper. This sets a great limitation on the options available to these people in their daily lives. People are being refused jobs because they cannot read well enough to fill-in or deliver an order to a customer.

As the persons with limited communication skills become older, it becomes increasingly difficult to admit to the lack of reading ability. As one 14-year-old said to me recently in a conversation, "It's really hard to admit you can't read when you're as old as I am." He is a child who has had a reputation of being disruptive in school and in the community. This raises the question of how one achieves self esteem when communication skills limit achieving esteem through the "conventional" means society at large values, means which require some "basic" skills of reading and writing.

Another young girl who is 15, said she did not need to know how to read. (She reads at a 4th grade level.) Her mother has six children by two or three different men, is a non-reader, and is on welfare. There is a strong belief in that type of setting that the women's role is to produce children. Their time orientation is one of immediate gratification—they do not worry about the future or the past.

Another set of relationships occurred for me in the League of Women Voters, a group consisting mainly of highly future-oriented college graduates. The contrast between these people and those cited above is fascinating to behold and to reflect on. An interesting dimension was added to this contrast when a research unit within the League closed and some members of the group found themselves applying for unemployment benefits and food stamps—things "those other people" do.

These examples highlight for me the differences in world view, normative beliefs, and overt behaviors, differing perceptions of intent and relationship, and certainly differences in code systems available for communicating. Furthermore the cases cited exist together within an area of 40 square miles and all involve Caucasians.

One problem of communication within small geographic areas is the assumption that the same approaches to communicating will work with all persons because they reside in the same geopolitical area and are of the same race. It seems we expect communication difficulties when we cross geopolitical, racial, or ethnic boundaries, but the difficulties may be just as great or greater within our own locales and within our own ethnic group.

Since the first edition of this book explicitly laid out a taxonomy of levels of interculturalness, more attention has been given to the notion of a continuum of interculturalness. I do not delude myself into believing that the change has occurred as a result of the first edition; hopefully it played a part. The change has been stimulated by many discussions that have been occurring within the field. But there is still reluctance to embrace this view in the study and practice of intercultural communication, at least that is my perception of the thinking in the field.

Gudykunst and Kim (1984) in their book, *Communicating with Strangers—An Intercultural Approach*, recognize communication variables and principles which cut across geographic, ethnic and racial boundaries. They even suggest the possibility of becoming an "intercultural person"—one who has developed special skills to adapt to differences and respond in situations of high uncertainty.

Some limited work was done by Suk Ja Kim, Melinda Lumanta, and Robert Roe (when they were doctoral students at Michigan State University) in developing and factor analyzing a set of world view items to place those participating in a communicative act along a continuum of homogeneity-heterogeneity on that dimension. It is the position along that continuum that determines the levels of interculturalness, hence the type of communication that is possible and the ease or difficulty with which it is carried out.

Suk Ja Kim collected a set of openended responses to questions in the three aspects of world view covered in this book—beliefs about nature of life, purpose of life and relation of the person to the cosmos. She asked persons in a midwestern university community: What is your view of the purpose of life? What is your view of the nature of life? What is your view of the relation of humans to the cosmos? the universe? When the responses were sorted and duplicates removed, 76 items remained. The world view dimension was selected for study first because it is assumed that this set of beliefs is the most stable and most resistant to change. Incidentally, these questions have provided a good base for opening discussions of world view in groups of varying ages and backgrounds.

Roe, Lumanta and Sarbaugh (1985), with help from Bernard Blackman of Florida State University, administered the 76 items to two sets of university students. The purpose was to see if the items would identify differing typologies of people on the world view dimension. One set of North American students at a midwest U.S. university responded in English; the other set in the Miami area were Puerto Rican students who responded to a Spanish language version of the 76 items. The English version was translated to Spanish and back, with checks by Anglo and Latin Americans fluent in both languages.

Using the Quanal Q-analysis program, developed by N. Van Tubergin of the University of Kentucky, Roe, and others extracted five people factors from the responses of North American subjects and four from the responses of the Puerto Rican subjects. The data also yielded 26 consensual items for the North Americans and 36 consensual items for the Puerto Ricans, suggesting more homogeneity among the latter group.

Dominant elements in the consensual items for the Puerto Ricans were that life was dull, monotonous, and meaningless. One of the five types of North American subjects expressed that same set of beliefs about the nature of life.

The consensual items for the North American subjects were: The purpose of life is to always do your best, whatever the situation; life is dynamic, always changing; life is fulfilling; and a person must learn to accept different opinions or ways of behaving.

Differences among the typologies tended to be along source of control dimensions, for example, control by a diety; controlling one's environment, including other people; or working in harmony with other sources of power.

You should not attempt to apply these specific descriptions to university students in general. They are a demonstration of what can be done in developing analyses based on the taxonomy. The consensual responses of the North American students may have been influenced by the process view of reality taught in the courses in which those students were enrolled at the time of the data collection.

The study did demonstrate that the world view items would group subjects in typologies according to their beliefs and that with the Quanal program, the differences among typologies could be specified. A five point Likert–type scale was used in collecting the data; but users of Quanal suggest that a Q-sort instrument or a 9-point Likert scale for data collection would increase the variance and provide sharper definitions of the typologies and the differences among them.

Confirmatory R-type factor analysis also revealed that 33 of the original 76 items would be appropriate for intercultural world view assessment. And of course, the smaller number of items would make data collection easier. Reliabilities for the 33 items were: Purpose of Life (15 items) a $=$ .873; Nature of Life (10 items) a $=$ .846; and Relation of Humans to the Cosmos (8 items) a $=$ .828. Those reliabilities were essentially the same as for the 76 items. The 33 items appear in Appendix C.

Using the taxonomy as a guide, John Brown-Parker of Australia, (1982 MSU dissertation) completed a study focusing on classroom communication. He was developing a technique for measuring adult education instructors' management of their verbal communication of perceived intentions in the classroom setting. Intention is a difficult concept to handle, yet it seems reasonable to believe that perceptions of the communicator's intent strongly influences responses to messages. Brown-Parker's study offers an interesting piece in the puzzle.

As a class assignment, I have asked students to apply the taxonomy to an unsatisfactory communication event in which they had been involved. In doing this, they were to identify factors which contributed to the lack of a satisfying outcome and recommend what could have been done to achieve the intended outcome. Nearly all students report new insights into the communication set which had resulted in an unanticipated and undesired outcome.

Perhaps the most dramatic result from this type of exercise was reported by a young American who had married a young woman from

Taiwan. They had met in Taiwan while he was working there, and came to the USA to live while he was doing the analysis. He said they had been having frequent communication and relationship problems although both were fluent in Chinese and English, both had some experience living in both societies, and both loved one another. Even so, they had been unable to establish any reasons for the difficulties they were experiencing. He said using the taxonomy brought into focus, for the first time, divergences of beliefs and expectations that were determining the assumptions from which they operated. Now, they discovered they could talk about the differences and resolve them.

Another doctoral student, a reading teacher majoring in education and linguistics, used the taxonomy to analyze the differences in world views of the students and the teacher in an elementary classroom. She did this when she began to think of the classroom setting as one involving intercultural communication. She said it revealed to her communication problems in the classroom that she had not been aware of before. It helped her specify the differences between the teacher's and the children's view of the world.

Experiences in using the taxonomy to analyze what occurred in communication breakdowns have shown its usefulness in alerting people to the types of complexities involved in all communication. If it serves to alert communicators to the various aspects of the process and how these are affected by increasing heterogeneity of participants, it will have served a useful purpose. With that information, communicators can prepare more effectively for the communication in which they engage.

Much more work needs to be done to determine the usefulness of the taxonomy as a research tool. The limited work done thus far offers promise.

Acknowledgments

My beliefs about intercultural communication are the product of so many conversations and activities with so many different people, in addition to reading, that it is impossible at this stage to identify who contributed what.

I owe a great debt to my students from Asia, Africa, South America, Europe, Australia, Canada, and Mexico, and to the Black and Mexican Americans who have been willing to share their thoughts about intercultural communication with me.

Then there are people like William Howell, Ed Stewart, Ed Glenn, Michael Prosser, Nemi Jain, Don MacDonald, Carl Couch, Alfred G. Smith, and many others with whom I have shared in conferences and committee meetings.

I want to thank Brent Ruben for encouraging me to write this book. My thanks, also, to several of my colleagues at Michigan State who have been most helpful in their suggestions and critiques of the ideas and the manuscript—Jack Bain, Erwin Bettinghaus, Bill Herzog, Iwao Ishino, Dick Martin, Charles Mauldin, Gerry Miller, Tom Muth, Joe Woelfel, Kevin Goss (Australia), Tom Mwanika (Uganda)—and numerous others who have been willing to listen and discuss the topic.

I am indebted also to James Stroup, speech communication teacher at Everett High School, Lansing, Michigan, and to international students with whom I work for their suggestions and criticisms in developing the dialogues in Chapters 5 to 10. My typists, Terrie McLeod and Ruth Langenbacher, were most patient and helpful throughout the preparation of the manuscript.

I share with all of these people the credit for what is good in the text; for the weaknesses, I accept sole responsibility.

L. E. S.

Contents

Introduction

The perspective of this book is predicated on the theory that the starting point for any event, including writing this manuscript, is arbitrary. Such arbitrariness is guided by the purpose at that point in time at which the starting point is designated. That perspective is part of the culture of the author.

To talk about intercultural communication requires some understanding of the concepts of communication and culture, and the interdependence of culture and communication. As part of the arbitrariness of the starting point in this manuscript, it is assumed that the reader has growing interest as well as some knowledge already in the concepts of communication, culture, and process.

The text will not devote much time to explicit conventional definitions of the concepts of communication and culture, nor to a discussion of the communication process. Information regarding the concepts of culture and communication and their interdependence will be implied in the text. Hopefully, the reader who wishes the conventional definitions of these concepts will seek them from numerous books on these topics. In one sense, the entire text is devoted to making explicit the conceptualization of communication and culture, and the interdependence of these concepts in all of human behavior.

To attain some commonality of approach to the text, some minimal definitions follow to provide a perspective on the use of these concepts in this text.

Definitions of *culture* abound in writings about human behavior. These may be found in writings of Ralph Linton, Franz Boas, A. L. Kroeber, F. Znaniecki, E. B. Tylor, Leslie White, B. Malinowski, A. R. Radcliffe-Brown, Ruth Benedict, Lindesmith and Strauss, C. Kluckhohn, A. I. Hallowell, and others. Influenced by reading the above, I look at *culture* as comprised by psychological, sociological, and techno-logical aspects.

1

When we say that persons belong to a given *culture,* we are grouping them with others who share common psychological, sociological, and technological trappings. More specifically, they share common world views; they have similar ways of relating to one another and organizing themselves in groups for interdependent activities; they have developed and use similar tools and instruments; their overt behavior in all situations is similar; and the symbol system (language) for carrying out interdependent acts is the same.

The *psychological* aspects of *culture* would include one's values, beliefs, attitudes, and concept of self; one's view of time and space; and one's relation to the cosmos and persons. The *sociological* aspect would encompass the geographic arrangements which are developed by two or more persons; and the positions, roles, and norms which have developed and are adhered to in relating to one another and meeting one's survival needs. The *technological* aspect includes all the artifacts which are used in providing shelter, food, water, ornamentation, recreation, health care, waste disposal, transmission of messages, etc. It should be noted that the three aspects of culture listed above are interdependent.

Communication is the process of using signs and symbols which elicit meanings in another person or persons. It has occurred when one person assigns meaning to a verbal or nonverbal act of another. The symbolic act may be *directly sensed* when the persons are physically together; or it may be conveyed between persons by some *interposed mechanism* or person; as with mass media, a runner, or telephone. The potential for communication is limited only by the boundaries imposed by our sensory receptors and the technology available to transmit codes over space and time.

The *interdependence* of *communication* and *culture* becomes apparent as we consider: (1) how unique communication patterns develop and get modified within each unique cultural grouping; and (2) that the uniformity of behaviors from one generation to the next is possible only through some means of communication. It also is apparent that communication is one means of initiating change in the ways of believing about and behaving toward the universe, including other persons.

Running through both concepts—*culture* and *communication*—is some notion of "commonality." The word communicate derives from the Latin communis (common). From this we may take the position that the communicative act involves achieving some commonness. It was noted previously that persons whom we designate as belonging to the same culture have several things in common. So, we note the element of commonality as being characteristic of both culture and communication.

Chapter 1 builds on that notion by using the concepts of *homogeneity* and *heterogeneity* to distinguish between communication, which we will label *intercultural,* and that which we will label *intracultural.* It will suggest that rather than a dichotomy between intra- and intercultural, it is more appropriate to think of level or degree of interculturalness.

Writings in cross-cultural or intercultural communication, often focus on cross-national or cross-racial communication. As Alfred G. Smith, director of the Institute of Communication Research at the University of Texas, points out, a transaction between any two persons has some aspects of intercultural communication within it. Even within the same family, there develop different norms, beliefs, social positions, etc., which complicate the transactions in which those persons engage.

One of the critical variables in any communication is the desire of the participants to successfully move from a state of independence to a state of interdependence, i.e., the desire to communicate. Obviously the desire may exist on the part of both participants in a dyad, on the part of neither, or within either of the pair and not the other.

Some discussion of the elements involved in moving from a state of independence to a state of interdependence will be found in Chapter 1. It is a description of that part of the communication process called openings by Carl Couch and his colleagues at the University of Iowa. Couch, et al., have been concentrating on a delineation of elements required to describe the process of communication. They have focused on the process as process.

The balance of Chapter 1 is devoted to suggesting some aspects of humans which tend to be universals and some which are highly variable among individuals and groups.

The thrust of Chapters 2 and 3 is to identify some key variables in communication; develop those into a systematic framework for classifying communication events; and use that scheme to identify the principles which apply to communication events within a given class or subclass of events. This would take the form of a taxonomy patterned after that employed by botanists, entomologists, and zoologists. Such a taxonomy should be an expanding system, deriving from sound theoretic principles capable of accommodating new events, and readily adaptable to increasing knowledge of the communication process.

With a taxonomy, of the type envisioned, it would be possible to categorize communication events according to their level of homogeneity-heterogeneity. The contention in this manuscript is that such a means of categorizing would be helpful in dealing with that set of events labeled intercultural. It should focus attention more forcefully on the critical variables, those which require different communication behavior in an intercultural setting than is required in an intracultural setting. It also should permit categorizing situations as having differing degrees of interculturalness.

In all candor, it should be recognized that the taxonomy developed here in no way approaches the level of precision of taxonomies developed for plants, animals, and insects. Botanists, zoologists, and entomologists have invested many, many more years of study in developing theoretically sound systems for their classifications. Numerous scientific breakthroughs along the way gave surges in the development and contributed to the usefulness and precision of those systems.

While recognizing that the present taxonomy lacks the level of precision and firmness of theoretic base that one might wish, it is hoped that the framework presented will be suggestive of new and useful ways of looking at intercultural communication. Hopefully, too, the continued study of communication will yield theories which will make possible more precise and useful conceptualizations and classification systems.

Chapter 4 presents a set of principles in the form of if-then, and correlational statements. These pertain to the variables which have been included in the taxonomy.

Chapters 5–10 present a set of cases to illustrate transactions at six different levels of homogeneity-heterogeneity. Chapter 11 provides some guidelines for the intercultural communicator, which includes most of us at least part of the time.

1

Some Boundaries for
Intercultural Communication

The latter part of the twentieth century provided one of the most spectacular cases of intercultural communication in the recent history of mankind. It was the contact, in the Philippine rain forest, between the Tasaday[1] tribe and the party headed by Manuel Elizade, Jr. of the Panamin unit of the Philippine government. One of Elizade's party referred to it as a strange sensation of traveling through time ... "a visit to my ancestors of 100,000 years ago." For the Tasaday, the shock of sudden exposure to twentieth century urban man and his tools must have been equally as great if not greater.

While the contrast in that case was both apparent and dramatic, the communication problems, in many ways, are similar to those among the inner city, suburbia, and a rural village in any country of the world. The task undertaken in this book is to identify and analyze the variables that affect the communication which we label intercultural, whether it occurs between individuals or groups, and in whatever geographic locale.

There appears to be a temptation among scholars and practitioners of communication to approach *intercultural* communication as though it were a different process than *intracultural* communication. As one begins to identify the variables that operate in the communication being studied, however, it becomes apparent that they are the same for both intercultural and intracultural settings. In all communication analysis, we are concerned with the characteristics of the participants, the relationships among them, their encoding and decoding behaviors, the channels by which they relay symbols to one another, the social and physical contexts within which they operate, and their intentions in the communicative act.

INTERCULTURAL AND INTERNATIONAL COMPARED

Sometimes intercultural becomes equated with international. This, of course, is too restrictive a view of intercultural. In both examples previously

[1] The tribe discovered in the Philippine rain forest region in 1971.

5

cited—(a) the Tasaday and the Philippine government team; and (b) inner city, suburbia, and rural village—the comparison is between cultural sets within a nation. From this perspective, international becomes a subset of intercultural.

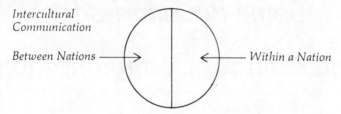

Intercultural
Communication

Between Nations ——————→   ←———— *Within a Nation*

There are two aspects of international communication which must be considered. One aspect is the communication which occurs between or among any two or more individuals of differing nationalities. The second aspect is that official communication, in which governmental representatives acting on behalf of their national government, exchange messages with governmental representatives of another nation, who also are authorized to act on behalf of their nation.

The level of interculturalness in any of these international transactions will depend on the kind and amount of expertise the participants have had with life in the other nation. It will be claimed here that some international transactions may well be categorized as intracultural, while others would be definitely intercultural. This could be true for either non-official or official communication.

Let's take an example in which international communication is not entirely subsumed within the intercultural. There are two school teachers from two different countries. Both have studied the same subjects under the same teachers in a third country; and both are now teaching agricultural irrigation in rural villages. Their cultural similarity has been further increased by extensive and intensive interaction as students so that they developed similar world views and beliefs while studying together. It is expected that their communication with one another will have higher fidelity and require less energy than will the communication of either of them with unschooled and unskilled workers in their respective countries.

The tendency to equate intercultural with international communication likely stems from the greater ease of identifying national boundaries. National boundaries somehow become more tangible than cultural boundaries; and, of course, there are noticeable differences in many aspects of behavior as one passes from one nation to another. There are noticeable differences also as one goes from a remote rural village in a country to metropolitan centers of that country. It's the differences between and among people, irrespective of geographical boundaries, that this text focuses on.

HETEROGENEITY—THE PRIME DISCRIMINATOR

A useful discriminator between intercultural and intracultural communication is the heterogeneity of the participants. The notion of "ideal types" (*see* Redfield, 1956) in regard to homogeneity-heterogeneity is helpful in developing this basis of distinguishing between intercultural and intracultural communication.

With the concept of ideal type, it is recognized that we would not expect to find two persons who were different on every characteristic; nor would we expect to find two persons who are alike on every characteristic. Yet it is useful to establish a continuum with the assumption of a pure homogeneous pair at one end and a pure heterogeneous pair at the other end.

Heterogeneous   *Homogeneous*
Participants   *Participants*

Intercultural   *Intracultural*

This view of intercultural and intracultural communication emphasizes that some communication events may rather easily be categorized as intercultural or intracultural. Others may be almost impossible to clearly classify as one or the other, i.e., those near the mid-point of the continuum. A perspective which classifies communication as either inter- or intracultural presumably does so using boundary criteria, either implicit or explicit.

The study and practice of communication can be approached with more precision if we classify it by level of interculturalness rather than as two dichotomous categories of intra- and intercultural. The initial difficulty will be to identify the critical dimensions of difference and to be able to specify the level among those dimensions a given transaction occurs at.

Another way of visualizing the inter-intracultural distinction (rather than the continuum) is to let two circles represent the life experiences of two persons (or groups). If the circles have minimal overlap (representing minimal similarity of experience), the two persons would be near the heterogeneous end of the continuum.

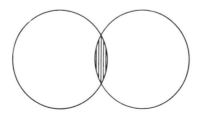

If the circles have maximum overlap, the two persons would be near the homogeneous end of the continuum, i.e., the intracultural communication end.

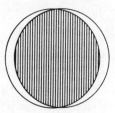

The homogeneity-heterogeneity distinction may lead to classifying communication across generations within the same village or town as highly intercultural communication. In societies where sex roles are quite distinct and clearly defined, there are aspects of intercultural communication in the communication between male and female. What is suggested here is that age or sex differences may or may not be intercultural. The classification of the communication as inter- or intracultural in this case will depend on what degree of homogeneity or heterogeneity of experiences the transactions of these persons have produced.

Still another way of expressing the distinction between intercultural and intracultural communication events, i.e., the boundary point on the continuum, is to say: In the intercultural situation, the variance in response between two persons to a given set of conditions is greater than the variance within either of the persons to the set of conditions over time. In the intracultural situation, the variance within the person may be as great as or greater than the variance between the two persons.

The Tasaday tribesmen and the Elizade team would represent two groups whose life-experiences barely overlap. The members of a close-knit nuclear family would represent a group of persons where the overlap would be maximal. Also, the Tasaday tribesmen would be highly homogeneous among themselves while members of the Elizade team would be quite heterogeneous within the team. The Elizade team was composed of Elizade, Charles Lindbergh, an interpreter from a tribe close to, but outside the rain forest, a hunter-trapper who lived part-time outside the rain forest and at times went into the forest to hunt, a U.S. newsman, carriers and some other support staff.

If we look at all communication as a series of transactions (see Wenberg and Wilmot, 1973), we then focus on the mutual involvement of the participants in delivering and receiving messages via whatever codes are available to them. The transactional view of communication emphasizes the mutuality of behaving either simultaneously or sequentially, the behavior of each influencing the behavior of the other. Speaking and listening generally are sequential, while behaviors involving nonverbal codes are more likely to be simultaneous.

If the focus is solely on speaking and listening, the act tends to be sequential in that one speaks, the other listens; the other speaks and the first listens. However, the production and reception of the nonverbal codes in a face-to-face situation will be occuring while the speaking and listening are occuring; and the parties may simultaneously produce and receive nonverbal codes with or without the production and reception of verbal codes.

As we describe and analyze transactions over time, we are dealing with communication as a process, not as a static event stopped in time. The interdependence of each participant with the other and with the environment is apparent in a process description.

Dan E. Miller, Robert A. Hintz, and Carl Couch at the University of Iowa have carefully studied what occurs in a variety of situations in which people initiate and carry on transactions. They started by watching what happens when two persons approach a door at the same time. How do these persons decide who goes through first? What are the various things that happen and in what order when two persons are in a room and only minimally aware of one another, then an emergency occurs outside the room? What are the elements of the communicative acts which follow? The assumption is that there are some universal principles here regardless of the level of interculturalness. Then, what are the differences in the operation or application of those principles with increasing heterogeneity (interculturalness)?

OPENINGS: FROM INDEPENDENCE TO INTERDEPENDENCE

Openings is the label which Miller, Hintz, and Couch (Couch and Hintz, 1975) give to the process by which transactions get initiated and move toward coordinated activity. For them, openings refer to the activities of two or more persons moving from a condition of behavioral independence to one of interdependence. It is thus the first necessary activity that two persons must successfully perform before they can do anything else together.

One of my African students told me that the most difficult thing for him to get accustomed to in the USA was the behavior of persons when meeting. In his country, if one person stopped, this was the signal for the other person coming toward him to stop for a talk. Here, he stopped and the other kept walking. This illustrates the necessity of the first element in the openings of Couch et al., i.e., reciprocally acknowledged attention.

The four elements of openings are:
1. Reciprocally acknowledged attention.
2. Mutual responsiveness.
3. Congruent functional identities.
4. Shared focus.

"Each of the elements must be constructed and maintained if concerted behavior is to occur," according to Miller, Hintz, and Couch.

We may use these categories in describing any communication transaction, whether intercultural or intracultural. It is a framework for studying communication as the process of two or more persons forming, maintaining, and dissolving unified lines of activity. These writers appear to have done what others have talked about, but few have done, i.e., study communication as a process.

If we were to look at intercultural communication from the perspective of "openings" we would expect that the heterogeneity among participants would complicate the efforts to carry out the four phases of openings. Work by Miller, Hintz, and Couch indicated that friend dyads accomplished openings in less than half the time that was required for stranger dyads. Three dyads of friends of long standing appeared to act simultaneously in accomplishing the four phases. In other instances the phases seemed to be sequentially produced.

When my African student is wearing the colorful dress of his country, other persons quickly and intensely attend to his presence. There is a high level of awareness, but the attention often is diverted away from the "opening" process in the transaction which he is attempting to initiate. The mutual responsiveness phase flounders. The African student and the other have difficulty anticipating each other. The transaction is different than intended by the student. They may find it virtually impossible to impute to the other sequences of behavior which are to follow, depending on the level of heterogeneity.

An Australian student reports that when he asks a question in class, all heads turn in his direction. He finds this very disconcerting, then has difficulty phrasing the question he intended to ask. As he speaks, the attention focuses on his Australian accent and the content of the question is missed. He reports that this has had a retarding effect on his asking questions about the content. There is an obvious lack of shared focus in this situation when the Australian starts his question. While the barrier may be overcome with increased time devoted to the transaction, it helps illustrate that the more intercultural the transaction, the more time one should allow for the satisfactory completion of it.

For any communicative acts to be established and to endure, a necessary first condition is that the parties attend to one another and acknowledge, either verbally or nonverbally or both, that they are attending. This is the first part of moving from a copresent social context to an interactive (or transactive) context. This is then a necessary condition for mutual responsiveness to occur; but as noted in the preceding illustration, it may not be a sufficient condition.

"One is responsive to another when he builds his acts off the prior, simultaneous or anticipated acts of another, and in the process of doing so informs the other participant(s) of that fact. Mutual responsiveness is obtained when each of the participants is in part organizing his activity on the basis of the other's activity and there is shared awareness that each is taking the other into account as they act toward each other and incorporate the other's activity into their own activity" (Couch and Hintz, 1975). Even to fight with another requires that each must be responsive to the activity of the other.

"Congruent functional identifies (the third set of relationships), are present when 'both parties mutually impute to self and other sequences of forthcoming behavior.'" The functional identities refer to doing something in relation to another person. "The identities become congruent when they fit together to allow for completion of what both participants recognize as a unit of social activity." My Australian student has learned to anticipate the actions of his classmates; the classmates generally are unaware of his adaptation; his class participation has declined and the communication process in the class has been altered.

The labels used by Miller, Hintz, and Couch are reasonably descriptive of the behavior. Shared focus, the fourth condition for openings to be achieved, is an object or event attended to by two or more persons with each aware that they are attending to the same object or event. This shared focus is the basis for a social plan of behavior to be accomplished through coordinated behavior.

As noted earlier, the openings are expected to take less time; they are more likely to occur, and are more likely to be satisfactorily completed among friends than among strangers. Further, it is expected that homogeneity will be greater among friends than among strangers. Thus another difference between highly intercultural and highly intracultural communication would be the ease and speed with which "openings" may be accomplished. It will be recognized that strangers, after some interaction, may discover that they are relatively homogeneous on many dimensions. But they start with less predictability than do friends, hence strangers are more likely than friends to feel ill at ease in establishing openings.

When my African student appears in a group of persons in the USA who have had very limited or no contact with Africans, the colorful dress immediately focuses attention on the differences. The fact that the African student attended a Christian missionary school for his elementary and secondary schooling, and has lived and worked in close contact with middle class families in the USA for the last three years is lost in the opening aspect of the communication process. Depending on the beliefs of the USA persons about Africans, the process may or may not move on from the reciprocally acknowledged attention to other aspects of the process—mutual responsiveness, congruent functional identities, and shared focus.

I would hypothesize that as visible heterogeneity increases, the reciprocally acknowledged attention will increase. That attention, however, may detract from the intended purpose of the transaction. Furthermore, it is expected that the communication difficulty would tend to increase as the heterogeneous participants proceed to each of the other three aspects of openings.

The participants may respond to one another, but the mutuality of those responses may be low as each misreads the prior acts of the other. The third aspect would likely be very difficult for highly heterogeneous participants as they attempt to impute to self and other sequences of forthcoming behavior. Each behavioral cue may suggest one type of forthcoming behavior to one participant and another type of forthcoming behavior to the other participant. The lack of fulfillment of the anticipated behavior likely would have a detrimental effect on the desire to continue the transaction.

When it comes to the fourth condition of openings, the shared focus, the difficulty experienced at the congruent functional identity phase likely will be further compounded. To have a basis for a social plan for accomplishing the desired coordinated action, the participants will need to have achieved a commonality of perspective about the way each should behave toward the other and toward objects required to achieve their goals.

One of the critical tasks is to identify the key variables (characteristics of participants and situations) which locate the communication along the homogeneous-heterogeneous continuum; i.e., the variables which influence the ease, speed, and fidelity with which the participants' move toward coordinated activity can be initiated and carried out.

SOME VARIABLES TO CONSIDER

Among the experiences of men everywhere are some which are common to all men. These may be taken as a base from which communication may be initiated; and they may form the base for "openings" at all levels of interculturalness and intraculturalness. Other experiences are unique to the members of each culture. These unique experiences are those which may be shared only through relating them to some common experience among the participants; this sharing takes longer and potentially is more likely to produce feelings of uneasiness among the participants.

Among the experiences which we would expect to be common to all humans are birth, growth, food, shelter, family, death, friendship, pain, happiness, motion, sleep, and natural elements—sun, moon, stars, plants, animals, land, and water.

Some elements such as rain and snow, will be differentially experienced; and it is extremely difficult for one who has experienced snow to communicate something about snow to one who has not experienced it. Obviously, the full experience of snow, as with most other phenomena, cannot be communicated apart from the direct experience of it. The completeness of communicating the experience of snow will depend on the number of other similar phenomena which the two persons have shared.

While we have listed a number of experiences which are common to all persons, the way in which these are experienced will differ among persons from differing cultures and among persons within the same culture. Note that the claim is being made that no two persons ever have identical experiences; and that communicating about phenomena apart from directly experiencing them will always result in somewhat different perceptions and interpretations. The more homogeneous the participants, the more similar the perceptions and interpretations following a communicative act; the more heterogeneous the participants, the more dissimilar the perceptions and interpretations.

Again, the operations of basic communication principles at different levels of inter-intraculturalness of communication is emphasized. The difference is one of degree rather than one of kind. We must keep that notion in mind as we now look at the characteristics which differ among individuals, resulting in different perceptions and interpretations in the communicative efforts. Note that the amount of difference will increase as we move from the most intracultural to the most intercultural communication act.

Among the characteristics on which we expect differences among participants in a communicative act are:

1. Language or code systems.
2. The beliefs they have about the world, the people in it, and appropriate beliefs and behaviors.
3. The perceived relationship between or among the participants.
4. The perceived intent of the other(s) in the transaction.

CODE SYSTEMS

Language is often thought of first as a critical factor in intercultural communication. This is quite natural since all of our transactions involve some form of verbal or nonverbal code. A shared set of verbal and nonverbal codes is a necessary condition for communication to occur, but it

certainly is not a sufficient condition. There is the possibility that the message, "we cannot achieve our intent," does come through when we have no shared code elements. Aside from that possibility, it seems defensible to say that some shared code elements is a necessary condition. The difficulty of concentrating on language differences is that the interdependence of language with other aspects of culture may be overlooked.

Every person who has had contact with persons from another language group has a repertoire of tales to tell; some innocent and humorous, and some of disastrous consequences. An often used example is that the O.K. sign in the USA means homosexual in some other cultures. Many nonverbal and verbal codes have perfectly acceptable denotations and connotations in one culture and may arouse offensive meanings among persons in another culture. There is no denying that language differences must receive special attention in intercultural communication, but one should also recognize that differences in beliefs about how people should behave are equally critical, if not more critical, in intercultural communication.

There is rarely, if ever, a one-to-one translation of codes from one language to another. Different cultures carve up the world in different ways and assign labels (codes or symbols) to the various elements in the physical and social environment. This will range from different categories of colors to different categories for ranking people within the group and different categories of roles.

Benjamin Whorf (1956) has claimed that one's language influences what one perceives and how it is interpreted. He has cited numerous examples to support that claim. One oft cited example is symbols for time in different cultures. Precise measures of time are very important to persons in highly technological cultures; while in the less industrialized societies there is less emphasis on time and the language codes are less precise for time.

Efforts to test the Whorf hypothesis with rigorous empirical research have not resolved the questions regarding the relation between language and perception of available stimuli. The more reasonable view would seem to be that there is an interdependence between language and what is in one's environment to sense.

We can observe that people create new elements in the language to label new categories of experience. Each of us also may note that we look at some aspects of our environment differently when our awareness is increased by new labels for events and relationships. For example, I became aware of different aspects of human relationship after being exposed to terms such as role, status, position, and norm in my first courses in sociology. Reciprocally acknowledged attention, mutual responsiveness, congruent functional identities, and shared focus also are having this effect as I work with those terms. They are suggesting a different way of looking at some aspects of communication.

Response to jokes is perhaps the best illustration of the inadequacy of learning the language of another culture group to insure effective communication with that group. We may notice the lack of response to jokes by two persons both of whom have learned the same vocabularies and grammatical structure but are from different cultures. The subtleties of intercultural communication are probably nowhere more apparent than in communication which involves humor.

For humor to be effectively communicated, the participants must share similar experiences in relation to the symbols being used. Since humor generally stems from a violation of expectations, the homogeneity of the participants in the communication must be sufficient to produce similar expectations about the object (or relationship) which is the subject of the humor. As the heterogeneity of the participants increases, the similarity of expectations aroused by a given set of symbols, tends to decline. Add to that, subtle (or not so subtle) differences in referent for a symbol used by both and the mutual responsiveness does not occur; one laughs but the other doesn't and can't see the humor in the message.

Within the consideration of symbol systems, we also must include beliefs and overt behaviors related to time and space. The literature abounds with examples of variations among cultures in regard to beliefs about and uses of time and space. Rather than take space here to provide another such inventory, some references will be included among the bibliographic items. Of course, one of the classics regarding time and space is Edward Hall's *Silent Language.*

PATTERNS OF BELIEF AND OVERT BEHAVIOR

Some of a person's beliefs may be unique to that person; others may be shared by all persons in the group or groups of which he is a member. In the latter case the beliefs take on normative characteristics with positive sanctions for adherence to the beliefs and overt behaviors accepted by the group; and there are negative sanctions for beliefs and behaviors not acceptable to the group.

One subset of beliefs will be given special attention, in the discussion of homogeneity-heterogeneity of participants. It will be called *world view.* As used here, world view encompasses that set of beliefs about the nature of life, the purpose of life, and the relation of man to the cosmos. The reason for handling this set separately is based on the assumption that this set of beliefs tends to develop more slowly and hence is more enduring than other beliefs. Further it is assumed that these world view beliefs are intertwined with beliefs about what is important or unimportant, what is appropriate or inappropriate.

World view encompasses the beliefs about where we came from, why we're here, and where we're going. It's the set of beliefs about how the human species fits into the overall scheme of things. It's the beliefs about death in relation to life; the belief or nonbelief in some kind of life after death; beliefs about controlling nature or being controlled by nature; and so on.

Another subset of beliefs singled out for additional treatment are those we call *values*. They include the beliefs about what is important or unimportant, good or bad, and right or wrong. They are broad and fundamental norms which are generally shared by groups. As such, they serve to guide, integrate, and channel the organized activities of the members. They are expressed in the norms of overt behavior and role expectations.

The role expectations are the anticipated ways for a person to perform in a given situation the behaviors associated with the position that person occupies in the social system. For example, it's the way others expect me to behave in my role as father, or teacher, or any of the other sets of behaviors for the positions I occupy within the social systems of which I'm a part. The normative patterns of overt behaviors under the heading of role expectations derive from the value orientations of the members of the group in which the behavior occurs.

If, for example, honesty is a strong value within myself and my group, and someone gives me too much money in payment for a service, then I'm expected to return the overpayment. It's part of the expectation of me in my role as a good member of the group.

When two or more persons are engaged in a transaction, they each may assume that they both know and both accept the same normative patterns of beliefs and overt behaviors. If they do indeed share the same patterns, the transaction has a better chance of proceeding efficiently than when they do not share the same patterns. When their beliefs about appropriate behaviors differ, there is a high probability of communication problems. One of my Ghanian friends provided a good example of this kind of problem.

This friend had told me that in several of the tribal cultures the authority figure is always accessible to all for whom he is an authority figure. A person who adheres to that belief may have difficulty adjusting to the Western bureaucratic cultural milieu where the authority figure is not readily accessible. An example of this occurred in my office.

A student came to see me in my role as assistant dean. The secretary told him that I was fully scheduled for the day and asked if he would like to make an appointment for the following day. The student said, "But, I'm here to see him now!" Each became very annoyed with the other. The student waited for an opportunity to be seen between the other appointments. The secretary later said, "I can't stand that Mr. Z; he's so demanding. He always thinks everyone else should stop and wait on him." The student also told me that he was having some difficulty with my secretary who was trying to keep him from seeing me. The secretary and the student had very different views of the appropriate behavior in this case.

Differences in patterns of behavior and belief among persons often are assigned stereotypically, based on what one has learned through all of his life experiences. People are responded to according to differences in age, sex, education, occupation, clothing, income level, etc., etc. There is a tendency to generalize that all assembly line workers, etc., will respond like all others in their category. There is some basis for such an expectation, since presumably they will have had an opportunity for similar experiences. However, this view overlooks the opportunities that individuals in each of those demographic categories have had for unique experiences.

Ideally, we would take into account the characteristics of each individual with whom we communicate; however, we often are forced to base our first predictions on some kind of general stereotype of the other person. Some of the old stereotypes that have interfered with effective communication and coordinated behavior are: all politicians are crooks; all French men are great lovers; all Indians are lazy and shiftless. In the process of interacting, reassessments occur among effective communicators so that more accurate judgments of and responses to the other person become possible. This assumes a dynamic, changing belief system, i.e., a process view of reality.

This view of the changes occurring during communication between two or more persons can be described by the concepts of assimilation and accommodation. These concepts are used in somewhat the same way as they are used by Piaget.

Assimilation is the process of exploring the environment, taking in parts of it, acting on those parts and transforming them into new forms which will fit into the existing structure. The messages in communicating represent the parts taken in. I may have been taught that good husbands are kind to their wives, but they don't do any work in the kitchen; that's "women's work." When I am in the Smith family home, I see Tom helping his wife Mary with the cooking and dishwashing. I can assimilate that experience into my belief structure which says that men should be kind to their wives. Certainly being helpful is being kind. There is some problem as far as the belief that men don't do kitchen work in their home. That requires making some accommodation in my belief system.

Accommodation, the complement of assimilation, is the process of adjusting the structure, the belief system, so that the individual's model of the world can accommodate each new acquisition. One's beliefs are built on these twin processes.

In transactions with heterogeneous others, there will be more new stimuli to be assimilated which in turn results in more accommodation of the belief system to new experiences. Both of the processes operating together produce progressively more stable equilibrium states of adaptation. Rigidity of the structure may inhibit the accommodation process, delaying the establishment of a new equilibrium, and thus interfering with intercultural communication.

If we reflect on the process of openings discussed earlier, it may be noted that the first three stages of that process are a necessary condition for the assimilation and accommodation to occur in transactions with any other persons; and that the process becomes more demanding with increasing heterogeneity between self and other. The shared focus is necessary for greater coordinated action and it also is more difficult to achieve with heterogeneity of the participants.

As one moves through life, even in a restricted physical and social environment such as that of the Tasaday, the assimilation-accommodation processes continue to produce new adaptations. Piaget states that life is a continuous creation of increasingly complex forms and a progressive balancing of these forms with the environment. For such as the Tasaday, these new adaptations may be more concentrated on experiences which we have listed as common to all humans.

When a party from Manila (or other urban center) enters the rain forest, many new stimuli are introduced to the Tasaday requiring a rapid change in the number and quality of events to be processed. As the accommodation is made, communication would become somewhat easier with those who have come from outside the rain forest.

The first efforts of the Manila party to communicate with the Tasaday achieved reciprocally acknowledged attention fairly soon, although the Manila party first saw the footprints and other signs of presence before a visible co-presence was established. The attention at first was focused on one another. Gradually as the co-presence in a mutually shared physical environment continued, there was reciprocally acknowledged attention; then it became possible to achieve mutual responsiveness, and finally some degree of congruent functional identity and shared focus. It required accommodation of belief structures by both parties before the new stimuli could be assimilated in the process of communicating. Much of the communication focused on those universal aspects of life noted earlier—food, shelter, family, etc.

One of the concerns of the Elizade party was the contamination of the Tasaday life style, a contamination which could never be retrenched. An ineradicable impact also had been made on the members of the Elizade party. In the few brief contacts between the two groups, some of the heterogeneity had been reduced; but it would take many extended contacts to change the world views of the two groups to the point that each could be reasonably certain that mutual perceptions and interpretations of phenomena were occurring. Throughout most of the world, the increasing access to mass media *is* expanding the range of contacts.

With the extension of television and other mass media, the potential for vicariously shared experiences becomes much greater for those persons who have access to the media. Industrialization has resulted in rather similar patterns of social organization and activities wherever it has occurred; thus, it has contributed to increasing the similarity of the beliefs.

Industrialization has made possible more rapid and more extensive travel with the concomitant opportunity for more persons to be exposed to more of the same phenomena. The process of industrialization and at least two of its products—high speed transportation and high speed communication over great distances for the masses—have contributed to a reduction of the heterogeneity of the participants in communication. But it would be unrealistic to assume that these processes would wipe out the difficulties of intercultural communication. It should help broaden the base within which effective communication can occur.

The beliefs about and attitudes toward persons from other cultures come from many kinds of exposure, both direct and indirect. If we begin listing how many of our beliefs are a result of our own direct experience, we find that many are relayed by other persons. Even the relaying may be indirect through printed or electronically recorded or transmitted messages. However acquired, these beliefs and attitudes serve to filter the stimuli to which we respond in our transactions with others and dictate the way in which we perceive and respond to those others.

Althen and Jaime (1971) in comparing Philippine and North American assumptions and values point out:

1. In North American culture, autonomy is encouraged; while in the Filipino culture, dependence is encouraged.
2. For the Filipino, there is a finite amount of good that can be divided and redivided but not augmented; thus, if one accumulates more wealth, he does so at the expense of others. For the North American, optimism exists that there is enough for everyone and the economics of self initiative is the arbiter of how much one accumulates.
3. For the North American, there is a dichotomy of work and play; for the Filipino, work and social life are not separated.
4. Confrontation in North America tends to be face-to-face; in the Philippines, it tends to be through an intermediary to avoid losing face.
5. The North American stresses the future; the Filipino stresses the present and the past, and life is lived from day to day.

These statements are based on some notion of modal characteristics of people of the two geographic areas. While we recognize that these comparisons will not hold for all persons in both areas, they illustrate some of the differences in values and assumptions about the world between two sets of persons from different geographic areas and different cultures, sets which are highly heterogeneous on some characteristics.

If Western time orientation and self advancement were relied on in efforts to encourage adoption of new technology in the Philippines, communication efforts would be very frustrating for both parties. The dictum of "know your audience," now broadened to "know the participants," which is referred to often in intracultural communication would be equally appropriate in this intercultural setting. The assumption is that if we will make the effort to know the beliefs and other characteristics of those with whom we are communicating, then we will be able to identify some shared foci for achieving coordinated action.

Different bases for assigning status and the violation of expectations as to how one responds to another of a different status often is a problem in intercultural communication. The trauma from the violation of expectations may block receipt of any other messages in the system. In this way, it precludes or at least interferes with establishing mutual responsiveness, congruent functional identities, and the shared focus of the Miller-Hintz-Couch model.

PERCEIVED RELATIONSHIP AMONG PARTICIPANTS

One of the places where this violation of expectation is most likely to occur is where one person who is accustomed to a strict hierarchical pattern of relationships is attempting to communicate with another who is accustomed to an egalitarian pattern. They will find that each has quite different expectations about what is appropriate behavior for the other. Embarrassment likely will result and may preclude effective communication on the intended topic. It may result from the use or non-use of formal titles by the egalitarian oriented person in referring to the hierarchically oriented person.

The difficulty of predicting social position, roles, and norms increases as heterogeneity of the participants increases. This lack of predictability creates tension and discomfort for both parties leading to embarrassment, perhaps hostility and a tendency to avoid further communication with one another.

A teacher in the USA may have a student from a traditional culture, such as Thailand. If the teacher is unaware of Thai culture, he may be disturbed by the lack of participation and the reluctance of the Thai student to ask questions. Later, after some months of acculturation, the Thai student may tell the teacher that students in Thailand are taught not to ask questions of the teacher, lest the question might embarrass the teacher. Here a different norm produced some stress in the relationship as the communication effort was not producing the intended mutual responsiveness.

PERCEIVED INTENT

The intent of the participants also influences the outcome of communication, regardless of the level of intra-interculturalness. If both have a desire to understand, to be understood, and to achieve coordinated action, they likely will commit whatever energy is necessary and undergo discomfort to achieve that goal.

One example of high energy commitment to achieve coordinated action is that of two persons (or groups) from different cultural backgrounds attempting to put aside previous antagonisms and work together on a common community program. It may require several sessions to assure one another that they can trust each other. They may have to ask third parties to confirm the positive intentions of the other, and each may have to take some risks of being criticized by the other. Each may have to admit previous errors of belief and actions toward the other, then show the seriousness of their new intent. Such admissions may be embarrassing.

If the intent of either or both parties is to obstruct achieving commonness of feeling and understanding, then either or both may refuse to expend any energy in the transaction. Ignoring the other is in a sense a rejection message. If the person being ignored perceives the intent of the other as rejection, then the person ignored may respond with hurt feelings, anger, withdrawal, revenge, or similar behaviors. It may be that the person merely had other items demanding attention at the moment and was not aware of not attending to the person who was feeling ignored. If both ignore one another, then there is no opportunity for coordinated activity.

On the other hand, each of us can undoubtedly think of cases where someone expended tremendous effort in order to deceive and otherwise thwart mutual understanding and coordinated action. This calculated deception may require more knowledge of one's audience than does the intent for cooperative, coordinated action.

The intelligence operations of unfriendly national governments in relation to one another is often one of highly sophisticated deceptions. In the case of two persons or small groups, it may be that one feels inferior, but goes to great effort through dress, limousines, and other status symbols to communicate that they are wealthy and of high status. When both parties in a situation are engaging in this kind of deception, it often becomes very humorous to an observer. It even becomes the basis for situation comedy in the entertainment media.

Another interesting case for considering perceived intent is the tourist from the USA buying some item from a street vendor who is accustomed to price bargaining. The intent of the vendor is to lower his price to about half the initial asking price. The expectation of the tourist is to pay the price asked. When the tourist pays the initial price, the vendor is surprised and may even be disappointed to have missed the excitement of negotiating the price.

In office situations, one employee may tell a supervisor that some of the work is low quality and that some action needs to be taken to correct the situation. On the surface, this seems like a strong intent to improve quality of output. The supervisor may or may not perceive that the intent of the

person is to criticize a fellow employee and perhaps have that person repri-
manded or negatively evaluated.

The sample of situations cited herein presumably will suggest numerous cases from your own experience where intent was correctly perceived
and cases where intent was incorrectly perceived; cases where intent was
positive toward you and cases where it was negative. You also can no doubt
remember cases where your intent toward the other was positive and cases
where your intent was negative.

In all cases, my perception of your intent will influence how I structure
my transactions with you, in my efforts to satisfy my needs in relation to
your intent. The accuracy of my judgments of your intent is expected to be
higher when we are highly homogeneous on the variables which we have
been discussing than when we are highly heterogeneous. Anyone traveling
in a strange country can report numerous cases of high uncertainty regarding the intent of persons with whom they were communicating. This is consistent with the general proposition that predictability of the other increases
with homogeneity of the participants and decreases with heterogeneity of
the participants; and that as predictability of the other increases, the possibility of achieving the intended outcome of the communication increases.

The next two chapters will take the variables discussed in this chapter,
explicate them more fully, and combine them in an effort to construct a
systematic schema for categorizing the homogeneity-heterogeneity of participants in communication events and situations. The schema is intended to
provide a useful base for analyzing communication situations to increase
the effectiveness of communicating. Included in that analysis is a recognition that participants in a transaction may be relatively homogeneous in
regard to one domain of meanings and highly heterogeneous with respect to
others.

EXERCISES

1. List the names of some persons with whom you frequently do things. These
   should be persons with whom you feel comfortable and enjoy doing things
   together.
   a. What characteristics do you have in common with them?
   b. In what ways do you differ from them?
2. List some categories of people with whom you have never talked or worked
   together on anything. These should be types of people with whom you think
   you would have difficulty talking or doing anything together.
   a. In what ways are you different from those persons?
   b. What characteristics would you and they have in common?
3. Which of the characteristics on which you differ from the persons listed in
   item number 2 do you believe would be easiest to overcome if you wanted
   to work on something with those persons in a mutually satisfying way?

   a. What would you most likely do with them?

   b. How would you cope with the differences in your efforts to communi‐
      cate effectively with them?

4. What are the pros and cons of the position that homogeneity-heterogeneity of participants is the main distinction between intracultural and intercultural communication?

5. What are the advantages and disadvantages of looking at levels of inter‐culturalness and intraculturalness rather than as two dichotomous variables?

    I hope you will check the answers you now give to these questions with suggestions you find in this text and with answers you would give after reading the text.

2

A Communication Taxonomy:

Its Value and Components

THE VALUE OF A TAXONOMY

The communication scholar is faced with a problem similar to that of the botanist, zoologist, or entomologist. Each has a tremendous number of individual items to study and explain in his efforts to plan and predict future behavior. If the botanist would attempt to do this with each individual plant, it would seem hopeless. If the zoologist would attempt to develop principles for each individually unique animal, it would be an overwhelming task; and the entomologist with the vast number of insects would have an impossible task if he approached each as though it were completely different from all the others.

Each of these groups of scholars has developed a systematic scheme for classifying the objects of their study. These are conceptually rigorous systems, taking into account variables which make a critical difference in the growth and development of each of the objects of study—plants, animals, or insects, as the case may be. Such a conceptual scheme allows more parsimonious theory development, hypothesis testing, and the generation of principles for the efficient propagation and care of beneficial plants, animals and insects, and for the eradication of those which man finds detrimental to his own growth and development.

If we can identify those elements which make a critical difference in the effectiveness and efficiency of communication among different types of persons in different types of situations, we can develop a systematic scheme for classifying communication events for study and management. The purpose of this chapter is to present the *beginnings* of such a system for communication. This system will be applied to our study of intracultural and intercultural communication. The hope is to produce a set of principles which can be used to improve the effectiveness and efficiency of all communication, and especially intercultural communication.

Efficiency, to me, implies the optimum balance between effectiveness and cost. The cost may be in dollars, time, or impediments to future communicative efforts. Effectiveness here is defined as the extent to which the participants achieve the intended outcome of the communication event.

24

The botanist, for example, will have a set of practices that apply to controlling growth for a category of plants which he labels legumes. One important characteristic of legume plants is the requirement of non-acid soil. Another category of plants will grow effectively only on acid soils. If it is known that a plant fits in the legume category, a program of treatment can be prescribed to produce optimum growth for it and all plants in that category. Such a system offers both parsimony and precise specifications for treatment.

The taxonomic scheme allows classification at a number of levels and with varying degrees of precision. With trees, e.g., one may start with the distinction between deciduous and evergreens. From this one may identify subclasses of each depending on their tolerance of or requirements for water, acidity, light, soil type, temperature ranges, chemicals, etc.

For the taxonomy to be theoretically and operationally useful, the variables that "make a difference" must be identified and combined to establish functional categories of objects and events. This is the primary challenge of the communication scholar in developing a rigorous taxonomy for classifying communication events.

The refinement of such a system is continuous, in that a first approximation may be developed with existing knowledge, then modifications may be made with each new bit of knowledge. Generalizations about communication will be derived for categories of events, i.e., people behaving in certain ways in certain situations to achieve certain outcomes. These generalizations would then be subjected to test for their validity and refined as indicated by the results obtained. This process will help determine whether the appropriate variables are being used to classify the events; whether the communication principles assumed are the appropriate ones to produce the intended outcome; and whether the principles are being applied appropriately to produce the most effective outcomes.

Consciously or unconsciously, participants in a communication event make several decisions. Among these are: physical location; the persons included and their beliefs, language and other characteristics; the use or non-use of interposed channels—electronic, print or other devices; the codes to use, either individually or in combination, judgments about the similarity or dissimilarity, among several dimensions, especially between self and the others who are involved; the intent of self and others; the preceding sets of events which impinge on the present situations; the positiveness, negativeness, or neutrality of the relationship among the participants; amount of time available; the "timing" of the communication in relation to the total context of events; individual feelings of comfort, stress, satisfaction, fear, sorrow, happiness, etc.; and judgments of the presence or absence of communication disorders, either physiological or psychological.

The number of combinations of those variables becomes staggering to comprehend and deal with. Yet, we do deal with them in some way every time we communicate, even though the "dealing with" may mean ignoring some of the factors mentioned.

THE SCHEME FOR CATEGORIZING

Approaches

One approach to generating categories for a communication taxonomy is to make a list of a large number of communication situations, then put together those which share the same characteristics. This is essentially the process of factor analysis in which those elements are identified which constitute a common factor.

An example of this approach would be to select from a listing of communication events those which involve only two persons in a private setting, using the same language, working to achieve a common goal, and where the participants had been close friends and had worked together for five or more years. This could be contrasted with a set of events which involved 10–20 persons in a public setting, using two or more different languages, facing a common problem but with different plans for solving it, involving persons who had never met before and where prior knowledge and beliefs differed and led to somewhat antagonistic and suspicious feelings toward one another.

In the example, the variables which would distinguish between the two sets of events are:

1. public vs. private
2. number of persons involved
3. intimacy of prior relationship and similarity of beliefs
4. similarity of language
5. similarity of goals

Among the five variables listed, it will be noted that the last three could easily be used to assess the level of homogeneity-heterogeneity among the participants. That would offer the possibility for classifying the first of the two cases above as highly intracultural, and the second of the two cases as highly intercultural.

This process of listing and separating the events into sets with common characteristics could proceed until a judgment was made that some optimum collection of meaningfully different sets of events had been established. The discriminating variables could be identified; then principles could be derived for dealing with communication in each of the various sets.

A second approach to generating a category scheme would be to list what are assumed to be the critical variables which influence communication outcomes and would thus be useful variables in categorizing communication events. These variables would be selected from those which have produced most notable results in prior studies. They also might be selected from those which come from speculation about the communication process; or a combination of those from speculation and those which past studies have indicated as useful in predicting and explaining communication outcomes.

A third approach is to work back and forth between the two approaches above, striving to develop an increasingly rigorous system through successive approximations.

I will start with a set of variables which I believe will be useful in categorizing communication events. From those, I will construct a general system for classifying these events, a rather crude taxonomy. Then I will take some situations and fit them into the system. The test of the system will be whether a particular communication is adequately described by one of the categories.

Any restructuring of a set of elements may be expected to provide a different way of looking at that part of the world. An outcome of a taxonomic system should be its power to generate an expanded set of generalizations and questions to guide communication behavior and study.

The Key Variables

Seven sets of variables will be used in developing the taxonomic system. These include:

a. Number of persons involved in the communication
b. Type of channels used
c. Perceived relationship among the participants
d. Perceived intent of the communicators
e. Code systems, including both verbal and nonverbal
f. Normative patterns of beliefs and overt behaviors, with special consideration of values and roles
g. World view as a special category of beliefs

It will be noted that variables *a* and *b* are situational variables which always influence the communication process, but influence it somewhat differently for different levels of interculturalness. Variables *c* and *d* also change from situation to situation; however, they are heavily influenced by the characteristics and behaviors of the participants themselves. Variables *e* to *g* inclusive are those which would be used to identify the level of homogeneity-heterogeneity of the participants.

It is not claimed that these variables are independent of one another in their effect, as has already been noted. It is believed that some understanding of each and its effect on the communication process will help communicators to better predict and explain the outcomes of their communication efforts. With that in mind, each of the variables will be discussed briefly here; then in Chapter 3 they will be combined into a taxonomic system.

With only two values for each of the variables there are 128 potential combinations for the seven variables. The potential number of values is obviously much larger than two. With only three values for each variable the number of potential combinations is 2,187; with four values, there are 16,384 potential combinations. Numbers such as these dramatize the magnitude of possible variations in communication and some of the complexities involved in studying the process.

To keep the taxonomy and the discussion of intercultural communication within some reasonably manageable frame, a limited set of values of the variables will be used. It will not be the same number of values for all variables; and some of the variables will be combined prior to building the taxonomy. As the explication of the variables develops, the basis for the combinations hopefully will become meaningful.

NUMBER OF PARTICIPANTS

Number of participants is a continuous variable ranging from two persons to an extremely large number. With worldwide coverage by electronic media, it is potentially possible to have the largest number of participants equal to the total population of the world. As this statement already suggests, number of persons is not independent of channels used in the communication process.

A tendency toward increased difficulty of communicating effectively is expected with an increase in number of persons involved. That increased difficulty is expected to be greater as the number of persons involved requires the use of channels which reduce either the immediacy of feedback or the number of sensory channels available. It also is expected that the increase in difficulty accompanying either more persons or less direct channels will be greater as the interculturalness of the communication situation increases.

Studies of consensus formation illustrate the increased time required to reach agreement on an issue as the number of persons in the group increases. Also, as the size of an organization increases, the complexity of the communication flow increases with an attendant greater probability of communication breakdowns.

It is conceivable that adding another person to a transaction may facilitate communication. This would obviously be true if two persons with two different languages were attempting a transaction and a third party is added who knows both languages. The third party may become an active participant in the transaction, or may serve mainly as translator.

The addition of another person or persons also may facilitate the communication when the added parties bring new information. This is especially true when the additional information is needed to achieve the goals of the participants.

We must be careful to recognize that the need for additional persons to achieve coordinated action and accomplish a complex task is not confused with the potential for communication breakdown. It is the added variation and the increased potential for distortion of messages which comes with the added variation that is being considered when the claim is made that there is a tendency for increased communication difficulty with increased numbers of persons involved. Furthermore, the sheer potential for each person to produce messages to which all the others may attend declines as the number of participants increases.

CHANNELS

It is readily apparent that the number of persons involved is not independent of the *channels* used. Especially in communication involving so many persons that a speaker could not be heard or seen, there is need for some form of *interposed channel*. An *interposed channel* is one in which some mechanical device or some person is between the primary participants to relay the messages. Interposed as used here most often will refer to telephone, broadcast media, or print media.

Direct channels are those in which the participants are in the physical presence of one another.

Channels for one-to-one communication may be either direct or interposed. A *direct channel* offers the most immediate feedback and the greatest choice of codes, potentially involving all sensory channels. An *interposed channel*, whether it is another person or some mechanical device, introduces some limits on the codes which may be used. Any *interposed channel* also is necessarily more restrictive of the context available for the interpreter of messages to use in his interpretation. On the other hand, new technology is making possible immediate feedback with 2-way simultaneous transmission via television, or phonevision. Citizens Band radio also is adding a new dimension to communication with ramifications as yet unknown. These still leave the problem of the more restricted context for interposed channels than for direct channels.

As noted earlier, the need for access to all possible code elements and for immediate feedback is greater as the heterogeneity of the participants increases, i.e., in the more intercultural communication situations. The feedback allows for more self-correction during the communication process; and the additional code elements permit each person to check for consistency among the codes employed by the other.

In the *direct channel* situation, one may use any of the five sensory modes, singly or in combination. One of the main advantages of the *direct channel* is the opportunity for using multiple sensory modes simultaneously. Which combinations are used, of course, is dependent on which senses are most appropriate to experience the aspect of the event one hopes to share with the other, e.g., hot-cold requires touch; sweet-sour requires taste, etc.

The choice of *interposed channels* again is dependent upon the aspect of an experience or event to be shared, the fidelity desired, the resources one is willing to commit, and the time and distance to be spanned. Both intuitive judgments and those based on empirical data, lead one who is seeking optimum effectiveness to use channels that can handle multiple sensory modes.

PERCEIVED RELATIONSHIPS

Perceived relationships between or among persons in a transaction will influence the level of trust or suspicion, anxiety or confidence, and the eagerness or reluctance to initiate the transaction. Three factors will be considered here which contribute to trust, confidence, and desire to communicate. These are: (a) the positiveness or negativeness of feeling toward the other; (b) the extent to which they believe their individual goals are compatible and mutually shared with one another, or are incompatible, and possibly conflicting; and (c) the extent to which they believe the relationship is hierarchical or equal.

One side of the perceived relationship is based on the view of people generally; the other side is based on knowledge of the specific participant. Some persons see other people as generally trustworthy, well-intentioned, worthwhile, and genuinely concerned about the well-being of those around them. There are others whose general view of people is so dominated by fear and suspicion that it borders on paranoia. This latter type believes that people can't be trusted; that people seek to manipulate and injure others whenever possible; and they believe people generally tend to be destructive, having evil intentions toward everyone and everything. Persons in this latter category tend to look at the relationship with others as one of "get the other guy before he gets you." This general view is a composite of judgments from one's experiences with people throughout his life.

A careful observer will be able to identify some persons in each of the two categories just cited; and they will recognize that there are many shades in between. It's likely, too, that most individuals will vary along this continuum as conditions around them change, suggesting that the perceived relationship between or among specific persons may change from time to time.

The positive or negative feelings a person has about himself often are projected onto other persons with whom he engages in transactions. I have found in my own introspections, perhaps you have too, that when I'm feeling unhappy with my own performance, I'm more likely to be impatient and critical of those around me.

For any given transaction, the participants will have as their basis for perceiving the nature of the relationship, their general orientation toward people combined with what they know about the specific persons involved with them. If they are engaged in a transaction with a person of another skin color than their own and all their prior experience with those of that skin color has been one of being dominated, they will have difficulty believing that the other person wants to operate as equals. Further experience with person A can confirm for person B that person A does intend to enter their transactions as an equal; then B can decide that it is safe to behave as an equal with person A with very satisfying results.

In intercultural situations, less specific data are available to the persons in the transactions regarding the other party. That leads to more reliance on the beliefs about people generally, and stereotypic beliefs based on whatever composite of experiences one has had with persons who appear similar to the other in the transaction. The perception of the relationship may be adjusted during the transaction depending on the nature of the mutual responsiveness, the congruence of functional identities and the shared focus which emerge.

The variable, *perceived relationships* (PR) between participants, is intended to be a composite of general and specific orientations toward one another. Under this variable, the positive-negative feeling dimensions will be categorized on a continuum of strongly positive feelings toward the other (F_1)[1] to strongly negative feelings toward the other (F_2).

The goal orientation dimension will be labeled on a continuum from mutually shared and compatible goals (G_1) to not compatible, not shared, and conflicting goals (G_2); and the hierarchical dimension of the relationship will be categorized along with the Watzlawick et al. (1967) continuum of symmetrical, i.e., not hierarchical (H_1) to complementary, i.e., strongly hierarchical (H_2).

Note that the labels for each of the dimensions of the perceived relationship variable identify opposite ends of a continuum.[2] At one end are

---

[1] The letters with numerical subscripts in parentheses beside the labels used in describing the variables are a shorthand which will be used in the statements to show the various combinations of variables in the taxonomy in Chapter 3. They are introduced here to help prepare the reader for their use later. The subscript of *one* (as in F_1) is intended to suggest homogeneity and ease of communication; and a subscript of two or more is intended to identify the level of variables where communication is expected to be more difficult, and involves heterogeneous participants.

[2] In selecting terms to designate polar ends of a continuum, often there are questions as to what are truly polar terms. Terms such as positive and negative generally are less troublesome than some other terms, with not positive and not negative being considered mid or neutral points on the continuum. Terms such as friendly and hostile are considered polar terms by some, with not friendly and not hostile being the neutral midpoint. Others may believe that these two terms are not on the same meaning dimension, with friendly and not friendly being a polar pair of terms and hostile and not hostile being another polar pair.

The pairs of terms used in this text to designate the homogeneous and heterogeneous poles of the variables have been checked by asking five to ten persons to name opposites in response to a question: What is the opposite of _____?

those which express perceptions which would encourage sharing of information $(F_1G_1H_1)$; and at the other end are those which express perceptions
which would tend to discourage sharing of information $(F_2G_2H_2)$.

It is possible, of course, for both persons to perceive a relationship in
the same way—positive feelings—sharing goals—symmetrical $(F_1G_1H_1)$.
Another possibility is that one person may expect the relationship to be an
$F_1G_1H_1$, while the other may see it as an $F_2G_2H_2$ relationship (negative
feelings, conflicting goals, and hierarchical). Still another alternative is that
both participants would see the relationship as $F_2G_2H_2$. It's also possible for
there to be congruence on the nature of the relationship on one dimension
but not on the other dimensions.

When I perceive the relationship to be highly favorable on all dimensions, I expect that the other will attend to me, have some concern with
helping me achieve my needs, will be kind, sympathetic, and understanding.
When I perceive that the relationship is very unfavorable, possibly antagonistic, then I expect the other person to be angry, unsympathetic, and unkind
or cruel with me, and that he will interfere with my efforts to satisfy my needs.

A symmetrical transaction is one in which the parties involved are
carrying out transactions as equals. Complementary (hierarchical) transactions are those in which one party is in a superior position and the other
is in a subordinate position.

If there is mutual satisfaction with a complementary relationship, the
communication may go smoothly; if there is dissatisfaction with the complementary nature of the relationship, the communication may produce
crossed transactions and game playing of the type described by Eric Berne
and others. In the negotiating situation there tends to be a desire by each of
the parties involved to control the complementarity of the relationship in a
highly competitive environment so as to put oneself in the favored or
dominant position. The desire to establish relational dominance may be so
strong in a transaction that all other messages are lost, i.e., not attended to
by either party.

The competitive-cooperative relationship involves the relationship
among the goals of the parties involved. In the competitive situation, the
goals of the parties are conflicting so that if one achieves his goal, the other
cannot and vice versa. In the cooperative situation, all parties are directing
their combined energies to achieving a common goal.

The combinations of elements under this dimension would range from
strongly positive feelings-cooperative-symmetrical $(F_1G_1H_1)$, to strongly
negative feelings-competitive-complementary $(F_2G_2H_2)$ at the other end of
the continuum. The contention here is that the last combination—strongly
negative feelings-competitive-complementary $(F_2G_2H_2)$—would be the one
in which the least probability exists for effective communication, the least
probability for either party to achieve the desired outcome. Conversely, the
first listed combination—strongly positive feelings-symmetrical-cooperative

$(F_1G_1H_1)$ would offer the highest probability of both parties achieving their desired outcomes from the communication.

PERCEIVED INTENT

Intent (I) of the participants in the communication is another of those variables which we take into account in our communication. Sometimes the intent of a communicator is conscious, definite, and explicit; sometimes it is implicit, indefinite, and ambiguous. There are persons who believe that the alternatives in communication are to control or be controlled. Darnell and Brockriede (1976), in dealing with intention and control in their discussion of choice and choice attribution in communication, offer a shared-freedom-of-choice model as an alternative to the control-or-be-controlled model.

I have approached the intent of participants in a transaction from introspection about my own intent in various situations. From this I have, for now, settled on the following categories of intent:

1. To share (s) experiences, beliefs, feelings, and materials.
2. To help (h) with a task, including dealing with feelings, questions, etc.
3. To ignore (ig) or avoid the other person, including his messages.
4. To disrupt (di) a transaction, or the efforts to establish interdependent activity.
5. To dominate (do) the relationship through "put downs", manipulating power, status, etc.
6. To injure (in) the other person or group physically, socially, or psychologically. This would include attacks on status, integrity, self-concept, etc.

I find that those categories encompass the more specific content of my own intent in a range of situations. Among those situations would be such desired outcomes as: to have you open the door (helping); to receive your suggestions about the usefulness of this taxonomy (share-help); to get answers to questions (share); to avoid a superior's attempts to embarrass me (ignore); to get the salesman to sell me a car at less than the usual price (dominate); to fire an employee (dominate); or to be flippant in a discussion where serious analysis might embarrass me (disrupt).

It becomes threatening to my self-concept to believe that I would deliberately communicate to injure another. However, an example of that might be the deliberate spreading of stories of indiscrete behavior of an opponent in a political campaign, or regarding someone I did not want in a responsible position in an organization.

Perhaps these are enough examples to suggest the base for the categories of intent of the participants which will be used in this taxonomy. In a transaction involving two participants or two groups of participants there would be 21 different possible pairings of those dimensions; i.e., sharing-sharing, sharing-disrupting, sharing-injuring, etc.

The greatest contrast would seem to be between a pair of participants who wish to share experiences, and a pair of participants who wish to dominate or injure each other. The interaction would likely be quite intense in both cases. In contrast, if the intent of both is to ignore the other, the transaction may be of relatively low intensity; it may not even achieve the first phase of an "opening", i.e., reciprocally acknowledged attention.

Some of the more frustrating communication may occur where one participant intends to share and the other intends to disrupt or ignore. It is suggested that when both parties have the same positive intent in engaging in a transaction, the intent is more likely to be realized. When the parties do not have the same intent in approaching the transaction, or where the intent of both is negative, there is a fairly high probability that the intent of one and often both participants will be frustrated.

The intent of the participants is more likely to be known in the highly intracultural communication than in highly intercultural communication. This claim follows from the contention that meanings are more likely to be shared when there is a homogeneity of code, world view, values, role expectations, and other normative beliefs.

In most transactions, intent is not explicitly stated. It generally is inferred from prior and present cues emitted by the other party. The meaning derived from those cues then forms the basis for the *perceived intent*, which in turn sets the tone for the communication.

If trust exists among the participants, an explicit statement of intent may reduce confusion regarding intent and facilitate effective communication. If trust does not exist, suspicion of intent likely will exist and be difficult to dispel; and the possibility of effective communication will be seriously impeded. Even in the latter case, an explicit statement of intent may facilitate further communication.

CODE SYSTEMS

The *code* (CS), both verbal and nonverbal, which each participant uses to elicit meanings in the other(s), is undoubtedly one of the most critical variables in all communication situations, at any level of intraculturalness and interculturalness.

One of the axioms of communication is that meaning elicited by a code—word, gesture, picture, etc.,—is unique for each individual in each context in which it occurs. The extent to which there is a consensual, similar or conflicting meaning elicited will depend on the extent to which participants have shared similar experiences in relation to the code and situation. This probably is the point at which heterogeneity of participants has the greatest impact in communication. The more heterogeneous the participants, the fewer experiences they will have shared in common, and the fewer experiences shared, the lower the probability of congruity of meaning elicited by a message available to both.

Not only are experiences different among heterogeneous participants, but those experiences likely will be categorized (conceptualized) differently. This makes it virtually impossible to have a one-to-one translation of words (and other codes) between language groups.

An experience from a study of dimensions of source evaluation among persons from two different countries (Sarbaugh, 1967) will illustrate this point. Some of the respondents from each country had been to the USA; the others had not. Those participating in the preliminary phase of the study were asked to list adjectives they would use in describing the best possible source of information for a question they had in their field of work. They were then asked to list adjectives used to describe the worst possible source. From 200 participants, 165 different adjectives were obtained. These were then translated into each of the languages, then back into English and back into the other languages.

The translators frequently pointed out the difficulty of finding suitable words to translate from one language to the other. One example was "scientific." The Ibo translators finally determined that the closest Ibo words when translated back to English would be "of this world." The Ibo words selected as closest to "unscientific" translate back into English as "not of this world." This is illustrative of the translation problem. The result was a set of 66 adjectives on which there was reasonably high agreement among three bilingual translators for each language.

Another illustration was shared with me by one of my students from Ghana. She told me that she has difficulty finding a suitable English translation from the Ghanian concept of "Asem No Apae." It's one of those situations where the equivalent notion is not common in "Western" cultures. It labels a situation where one person has offended or done some wrong to another. The situation is brought to the chief or a court of elders. Literally, the words translate into: "The matter has divided into two equal parts." There are no guilty parties. It is to be settled between the parties themselves by agreeing that they both should forget and proceed as though it never happened. This case also illustrates those situations where the language is not readily translatable due to differences in norms and role expectations between the two language groups.

To be an effective translator of codes between two distinct cultural groups, one would need to have been immersed in both cultures. Such a translator would have an appreciation for the subtleties of meaning elicited by the codes and would select codes in the second language which would elicit meanings closest to the meanings intended by the person whose code he is translating. Four combinations of knowledge of codes which may exist between persons who are communicating are used here:

a. Both (or all) individuals in the situation share a common code, i.e., Person A and Person B know and share a common code system. In the shorthand, this will be CS_1.

    b. Person A knows code 1, but not code 2; Person B knows code 2 but not code 1. This type of situation will be labeled CS_3.

    c. Person A knows codes 1 and 2; Person B knows only code 2. The reverse of this where Person B knows both codes and Person A knows only one would operate in the same way. The situation falls between a and b and will be labeled CS_2.

    d. Both sharing two codes is an elaboration of situation a above and also will be identified as CS_1.

Situation a or d is necessary for those communications we would label intracultural. However, as has already been suggested earlier, sharing a common code may not be sufficient to provide communication that we would label intracultural. Differences between the participants on dimensions other than code may be great enough to interfere with achieving a desired state of interdependence. In that case, even though the participants know the same codes, the communication will be near the intercultural end of the continuum.

Situation c may be only minimally intercultural. The person who shares both codes may communicate with the other using the code which is common to both. If they are relatively homogeneous on the other dimensions presumed critical in effective communication, then the code would not be a critical deterrent in this situation. There may be some nuances of meaning on the part of the person with the two codes which could not be shared since one person lacks one of the systems for categorizing some aspects of reality which the other has available for use.

Situation b would be the one which would cause the most difficulty in communicating. A third party translator could help bridge the code gap. However, if we accept a whorfian (Whorf, 1956) position that one's code influences the way one structures reality, then we would expect differences on some of the other variables. If by chance, there is relatively high homogeneity on the other variables, a third party translator likely could help the persons overcome the code difference and communicate effectively. In the highly intercultural situation, if the translator has been immersed in both cultures, the heterogeneity gap between the parties wishing to communicate may be handled reasonably well; however, it will require considerably more time and energy to achieve effective communication.

Without the aid of the translator, the parties may find some points of commonality which will permit some interdependent activity. It will require more time and energy and the level of certainty of what has been shared will be very low, in most cases.

One of the memorable experiences my wife and I had during a visit to Venice, Italy, was buying a shirt for our daughter from a shopkeeper who spoke no English. Our 100-word Italian vocabulary did not include words to refer to the characteristics of shirts which we wanted to know about before buying. With the aid of a pocket dictionary and much sign language we learned that the fabric was machine washable, did not require ironing, that it was a synthetic fabric (a type unknown to us) and we managed to get the correct size. This transaction required 20–30 minutes to complete. It's an example of a highly heterogeneous code combination, CS_3.

The four combinations of knowing codes cited above presume reasonably high proficiency in the codes known by the participants. If the varying levels of facility and sophistication with a code are added to the dimensions cited, the number of levels of similarity-dissimilarity increases fantastically. That's a further refinement that could be handled after the first assessment of homogeneity-heterogeneity.

For relatively simple transactions dealing with fairly concrete acts, the parties can achieve mutual satisfaction of their needs with lower language facility than when the transactions deal with highly complex and abstract notions. We satisfactorily bought the shirt from the Italian shopkeeper; but we would not have had much success attempting to discuss the ramifications of the divorce referendum which was being voted on in Italy at that time.

The more abstract the communication content, the higher the level of uncertainty at all levels of interculturalness, but the uncertainty will be much higher in the highly intercultural communication and the probability of satisfactorily reducing that uncertainty will decline as the heterogeneity increases.

NORMATIVE BELIEFS AND OVERT BEHAVIORS

Norms are the standards for beliefs and behaviors that develop within any group which we consider a culture or subculture. For our purposes the normative continuum for behaviors and beliefs ranges from *"must do"* to *"must not do,"* with those in the middle range being *"allowed."* The behaviors and beliefs at the two ends of the continuum are highly obligatory, with maximum flexibility and freedom for those behaviors and beliefs at the midpoint.

There are *norms* for what one wears on what occasions, how close one stands or sits to other persons for given activities, when to speak or not speak, which words to use when and where, what to eat and how, what time to arrive for visits, how long to stay, how one works, etc.

The content of values is normative in nature. There are certain values that one must hold to be a member of a culture; and there are values that must be rejected, as well as some that are allowed. Hence, values are part of the normative structure; and they will be discussed later in this chapter.

Taboos are *norms* of the very strong "must not do" type. Gantz (1975) has developed one of the more precise ways of looking at taboo communication. He lists three types of taboos—overt behavior, communicative, and

both communicative and overt behavior. He also points out that taboos are
bound by time, setting and participants. It should be recognized that what is
taboo in one culture may be common practice in another; e.g., the eating of
pork or beef.

A more specific statement of *types of taboos* would include:

a. Behaviors which are neither *talked about* nor *done* (e.g., sex relations
   with one's parent).
b. Those which are *talked about* but *not done* (e.g., eating of some foods
   such as snakes or ants in some cultures).
c. Those which may be *done* but are *not talked about* (e.g., sex relations
   between marital partners).
d. Those which may be *talked about in one setting*, but *not in another*
   (e.g., your physician may talk with you in his office about your urina-
   tion problems, but not at a party).
e. Those which may be *done in some settings* but *not in others* (e.g., in
   the USA it is permissible for a male to be in a room nude with his wife
   or his brother, but not with both present).

Many taboos develop around sexual behaviors, other biologic functions, and around patterns of interpersonal relations. They tend to relate to
those behaviors which affect the well-being and stability of the society.

One of the grave risks in intercultural communication is that of violating taboos. Knowledge of and adherence to norms, especially those of the
obligatory "must-must not" levels, is one of the very important requirements for effective communication.

In communication, between homogeneous participants, both, by
definition, will know and adhere to the norms. The levels of knowing and
adhering to norms used in this text will be outlined in the next chapter.

Norms form the standard set of rules for belief and overt behavior for
all persons in a given society. To the extent that norms are known and adhered to among a given set of persons, their beliefs and behavior become
more predictable.

Values, in keeping with the theme of this text, are of concern in relation to their similarity or dissimilarity among the participants in the communication. This similarity would apply to both the content and structure (Kohlberg, 1975) of the values.

There are numerous definitions of values, as with most social science concepts. Values, as used here, will be that set of beliefs about what is important or unimportant, good or bad, right or wrong. It's the set of beliefs that strongly influence what one does or refuses to do; and when, how, and with whom one does those things.

Knowing and accepting the values of the other would contribute to the homogeneity of the participants, while not knowing and not having similar values would contribute most to the heterogeneity of the participants. Presumably the first situation would be the most conducive combination for effective communication, while the latter situation would be least conducive. Where participants have similar values, but don't know that they do, it is assumed that the participants could discover through their transactions that they do indeed share similar values; then they could proceed with their communication from a common frame of reference.

The reasoning is that when the values of the other are *not* known, many more untested assumptions are operating within the communication. Not knowing increases the risks of inappropriate decisions in starting and carrying out transactions. More time is required in testing these assumptions before the intent of the transaction can be approached, unless the intent is merely to test the assumptions of similarity or dissimilarity. Keep in mind that honesty may be a value for both participants, but what constitutes honesty may differ between them.

The extent to which differences in values of the participants will be a barrier to communication will depend on whether they share a value which holds that one ought to tolerate and adapt to differences in persons with whom one is involved in a transaction. This tolerance offers some potential for establishing interdependent activity. Of course, this tolerance itself indicates some level of shared values. Where the values are different and the tolerance of difference in values is lacking, there may be little desire to communicate; and where communication is required, it is not likely to be effective or satisfying.

Where it is merely a matter of the values not being known, this may be overcome by communicating. Values of other participants also may be learned from sources who know the values of those with whom you will communicate. Obviously, an inventory of values of all the various cultural groupings and subgroupings would be overwhelmingly encyclopedic. On the other hand, there are some broad classifications which provide a useful starting point in knowing the values and other characteristics of persons from another culture. Such a starting point can facilitate that initial communication intended to increase the knowing.

Sitaram and Cogdell (1976) provide a useful comparison of values generally held by members of five different "cultures"—Western, Eastern, Muslim, African, and American blacks. Their tabulation of 28 societal values, such as individuality, equality of women, education, modesty, peace, authoritarianism, etc., focuses on values content as do most writings on values clarification. Such classifications are helpful to a person who will engage in communication with a person from one of those broad cultural areas. It will provide a basis for an initial assessment of the similarity or dissimilarity, and the nature of the dissimilarity, where it is dissimilar.

What Kohlberg refers to as the structure of values is another aspect which will influence the effectiveness of the participants in a communicative effort. For Kohlberg, there are three levels and two stages within each level from which one approaches moral judgment. These levels identify the structure. They are an outgrowth of his effort to validate, through longitudinal studies, levels and stages of value development set forth by Dewey and Piaget.

Level one for Dewey and Piaget was a *premoral* or *preconventional* level. For Dewey, behavior at this level was motivated by biological and social impulses; for Piaget, level one persons had no sense of obligation to rules. Level two people for Dewey were at a *conventional* level in which the individual accepts the standards of his group with little critical reflection. Piaget's level two is labeled a *heteronomous stage* whre "right" is a literal obedience to rules and obligation is equated with power and punishment. Level three for Dewey is an *autonomous* level in which conduct is guided by the individual thinking and judging for himself whether a purpose is good. Piaget's level three also is labeled *autonomous*. Here the purposes and consequences of following the rules are considered, and obligation is based on reciprocity and exchange.

Kohlberg (1975) labels his three levels (a) *preconventional*, (b) *conventional*, and (c) *postconventional, autonomous,* or *principled.* At the *preconventional level*, the person is responsive to rules and labels of good-bad, right-wrong, but interprets these in terms of physical or hedonistic consequences, or the power of those who set forth the rules and labels.

Stage one of the preconventional level is a punishment-obedience orientation; avoidance of punishment and unquestioning deference to power are valued in their own right. *Stage two* is an instrumental-relativist orientation; right action is that which satisfies one's own needs; reciprocity is a matter of "you scratch my back and I'll scratch yours."

At the *conventional level*, the maintenance of the expectations of the family, group, or nation is valued in its own right. There is not only conformity to personal expectations and the social order, but loyalty to it. *Stage three*, the first stage within this level, is a "good boy-nice girl" orientation in which good behavior is that which pleases or helps others and is approved by them. *Stage four* is a law and order orientation. This is an orientation toward authority, fixed rules, and maintaining the social order. Right behavior consists of doing one's duty, respecting authority, and maintaining the social order for its own sake.

Level three, the *postconventional, autonomous,* or *principled level* is one where there is an effort to define moral values and principles apart from the authority or identification with any particular group. *Stage five,* the first stage within this level, is a social contract, legalistic orientation. Right action tends to be defined in terms of general individual rights and standards which have been critically examined and agreed upon by the whole society. There is an emphasis on a legal point of view but with the possibility of changing law within a framework of rational consideration of social utility.

Stage six is the universal-ethical principle orientation. Right is defined by a decision of conscience in accord with self-chosen ethical principles appealing to logical comprehensiveness, universality and consistency. Examples are the Golden Rule, or Kant's categorial imperative ("Choose only as you would be willing to have everyone choose in your situation;" and "act always toward the other as an end, not a means"). These contain the dual criteria of universality and respect for the human personality.

An illustration may help to distinguish between the content and the structure of values. I have a value which says it is wrong to steal anything from another person or organization. The content is: "It's wrong to steal." The structure will indicate the level at which I operate in following that value. Level one would say I might be caught and punished, so I won't steal if there's a risk of being caught. Level two would say it's not in keeping with the rules of society and as a loyal member of society, I won't steal because it's not good for society. Level three would ask, would I choose to have someone steal from me if the situation were reversed. It also would ask what the consequences are for me and for other persons in the short-range and in the long-range. Are there conditions under which stealing might be acceptable; e.g., if it were the only way to save a person's life? What is the higher principle that would determine the decision and the conditions under which one might steal, if ever?

If two persons, or two groups of persons are operating with different value orientations, either of content or structure, their communication would be much more difficult and more subject to breakdown than if they were operating at the same level. One who is aware of the different value levels would have some advantage over the person who is unaware; but even awareness of the levels would not seem to be enough to overcome the barriers introduced when the other participant is operating at a different level of values.

The contention here is that the similarity or dissimilarity of value structure (the levels) among the participants, in addition to the values content, will influence the outcome of the communication. It's another of the dimensions which establishes level of homogeneity-heterogeneity, hence, the extent to which the communication is intercultural.

Roles, as *sets of shared expectations* about how one behaves in a given situation, are another critical aspect of intercultural communication. The participants in a communication constantly adjust and readjust their behavior toward one another. This is what Mead (1934) and others call "taking the role of the other." To do that in a way that leads to effective communication, one must have a reasonably accurate knowledge of the expected behavior for both parties in the situation.

In the homogeneity-heterogeneity model being developed, the homogeneous participants would be those who know the expected role behaviors in the situation and can respond appropriately to the behavior. The extreme of heterogeneity exists when the participants do not know the expected role behaviors and their "guestimates" are inaccurate. The result in the heterogeneous (intercultural) case is likely to be noninterpretable or misinterpreted adjustments to one another and an inability to achieve intended outcomes.

Mead's generalized other is the generally uniform set of behaviors which one member of a culture (homogeneous group) expects of other members of that culture in given situations. Based on my playing of the roles in which I operate day-by-day and on the way I observe others in similar positions play those roles, I arrive at this generalized picture of the expected behavior in the various situations in which I find myself. I then develop the expectation that all persons occupying similar positions in my society will play those roles in much the same way, or at least within some reasonably well-defined boundaries.

In a given week, I play the roles of husband, father, teacher, administrator, neighbor, choir member, shopper, member of selected organizations, committee member, etc. To the extent that I and others share the same beliefs about how I should behave in those roles, we will be able to communicate more effectively than if we held divergent beliefs about the expected behavior.

It is fairly obvious that roles come in pairs. For me to be a father, there is a son or daughter; for me to be a husband, there is a wife, etc. It is the set of reciprocal relationships which are created by communication and in turn affect the communication which occurs.

The various combinations of knowing and adhering to the same or different definitions of roles and other normative beliefs will be presented in Chapter 3.

WORLD VIEW

World View (WV), a variable considered helpful in assessing homogeneity-heterogeneity among participants, is used here to refer to one's view of the *purpose of life* (PL), the *nature of life* (NL), and the *relation of man to the cosmos* (RMC). It would include the belief or nonbelief in a deity; and if a belief in a deity, the nature of the deity.

The *nature of life* (NL), for some people, is continual drudgery, pain, and suffering. It's something to tolerate rather than enjoy. For some, this comes out of a set of religious beliefs which claim that man was born in sin and condemned to continual suffering; that the purpose of life is to prepare for some utopian life after death. For others life is a continual process of growth, full of anticipation, discovery, and the possibility of improving the comfort and enjoyment; life is a cyclical process of regeneration, maturation, decline (deterioration), regeneration, etc. Questions of mind, body, and soul are aspects of the beliefs about the nature of life.

For the physiologist, the nature of life may be described in terms of cells and the processes by which cells combine, divide, grow and die. It may involve questions regarding the set of conditions for life to begin and life to end, and the search for a definition of "life."

Some persons view life and the various events in the world as deterministic and quite predictable. For other persons, life and all aspects of the universe are in a constant state of flux, and any predictions are more or less probable of being confirmed. Different perspectives on the nature of life between or among persons contribute to different world views among those persons.

The *purpose of life* (PL) for one set of persons may be to control as many things and to accumulate all the resources possible for their own pleasure, irrespective of other persons now or in the future. For another set of persons, the purpose is to live modestly, to strive to know God's will and live as God directs, recognizing that everything is in God's hands. For still another set, there may be a recognition of some all encompassing force, and the purpose of one's life is to develop scientific laws which specify the relationships among forces emanating from that all encompassing force; strive to have all persons understand the long-range consequences of various courses of action; then select those courses of action which will benefit most persons now and in ages to come. These and other different views of the purposes of life would identify another aspect of heterogeneity and an aspect of intercultural communication.

The *relation of man to the cosmos* (RMC) could be one of being subjugated to the cosmos, hence helpless; or one of working with nature to preserve and improve the products of the cosmos for the ultimate benefit of man and other elements in the cosmos in a continuing state of balance and renewal; or one of man controlling nature for his own benefit, assuming that unlimited resources will continue to be available to man to use.

When persons who have different views of this relationship of man to the cosmos attempt to communicate, they will be expected to experience

Man Subjugated to Nature

Man With Nature

Man Over Nature

communication difficulties. They will be looking at the world from different perspectives and may have difficulty appreciating the different assumptions from which the other is operating.

Time orientation is an important aspect of *world view* (WV) which impinges on communication and other coordinated activities among persons. For some persons, the past is the most meaningful aspect of life and the preservation of past traditions is highly valued. For another, the anticipation of the future offers a very satisfying excitement; and preparation for the future includes efforts to modify the past, consuming much energy of both thought and overt acts. For still others, the emphasis is on the present; some in a self-indulgent way that attempts to ignore future or past. For still others, there is an orientation which some have labeled the self-actualizing orientation (Johnson, 1972); it emphasizes living in the present with a strong appreciation of and involvement in both past and future orientations.

Time orientation, as viewed here, becomes intertwined with views of the nature and purpose of life and of man's relation to the cosmos. As noted above, as the dissimilarity increases among persons in these various components of what is here called world view, the transactions among those persons will become increasingly more difficult. As noted in the illustrations in Chapter 1, the transaction among heterogeneous participants may achieve reciprocally acknowledged attention; but achieving mutual responsiveness, congruent functional identity, and shared focus is highly unlikely with the increased heterogeneity.

Some people may seek to avoid thinking about the nature and purpose of life and man's relation to the cosmos. They might find any reflection on questions of that sort very frustrating and disturbing. Others might enjoy such reflections and seek discussions with others about such topics. One might focus almost solely on physical gratification; another would focus on self-denial in regard to physical gratification and see the purpose of life as achieving some ultimate state of self-denial. Some would say that it is not for man to know either the nature or purpose of life.

Some people might believe that the spirits of their ancestors are within them and control their behavior. Others feel a nearly complete independence of ancestors and are proud of their difference from their ancestors.

All of the possibilities suggested above represent some of the dimensions along which participants in a transaction may differ on the variable which I've called *world view* (WV).

STABILITY OF THE VARIABLES

Among the variables which pertain to characteristics of the participants, two seem most likely to be dynamic and changing. These are the perceived relationship among the participants and their intent. As the participants engage in communication, they may find the relationship of each to the other changing and they may clarify or agree to change their intent.

Beliefs pertaining to world view and values are expected to be the most stable, most enduring, and slowest to change of any of the variables. These beliefs are built up slowly and continuously, with repeated reinforcement, throughout one's lifetime. It is recognized that they do change, but they represent generally highly ego-involving beliefs; and it is recognized that the greater the ego-involvement with a belief, the more resistant to change it is likely to be.

Codes, role prescriptions, and normative beliefs, other than values and world view, are relatively stable; but they are expected to be more likely to change than are world view and values. There is evidence all around us, especially from generation to generation, of changes in language—both verbal and nonverbal. As new technology develops, it brings new codes, new positions and roles, and new knowledge to assimilate ir our belief system.

This view of the stability of the variables would suggest that if one wanted to modify a communication situation so that it would be at a more efficient level, the first variables to manipulate would be the channel and number of persons. The next level which one might affect would be perceived intent and relationship.

As we seek to modify those variables which deal directly with the homogeneity-heterogeneity of the participants, the code and role expectations would be easiest to affect. Values and world view would seem to be the most difficult to modify. Over an extended time, repeated transactions would likely lead to greater homogeneity in values and world view among initially heterogeneous participants. This latter possibility offers the potential for highly heterogeneous communicators to increase the effectiveness and efficiency of their communication.

EXERCISES

1. (a)   Pick a communication situation in which you found yourself within the past week, one in which you felt communication was highly efficient. Write the description of that situation using the variables from Chapter 2.
   (b)   Pick a second communication situation in which you were involved within the past week, one in which you felt the communication was very inefficient. Write the description of that situation using the variables from Chapter 2.
   (c)   Which elements are different in the two situations you described?
2. (a)   What, if anything, could you do to change situation 1.b to get greater efficiency of communication?
   (b)   What elements would you change?
   (c)   How would you go about changing them?
3. (a)   What communication principles can you generate from your experiences in the two situations?
   (b)   What principles would you apply in a similar situation in the future?

You may include here the principles that you know from your study of communication, as well as those you may have generated from your own introspection and analysis.

Try stating the principles in terms of "If . . . , then . . ." propositions. For example: If the number of persons in a communication situation is increased, (then) the time required to achieve consensus will tend to increase geometrically.

I hope you'll keep your list of principles and compare it with those you think would apply after you have finished the text.

3

A Communication Taxonomy:

Its Structure

Having decided upon the key variables to be considered in the discussion of intercultural communication, the task now is to combine them to form the taxonomic structure. The combination will then be used to rank levels of interculturalness. This is the function of the taxonomy in this text.

The combinations of the various values of the variables will produce categories of communication situations. These categories will emphasize different degrees of similarity and dissimilarity of the participants. This will provide the base for ranking levels of heterogeneity and homogeneity of the participants with different numbers of persons involved and with different channels being used.

To create a statement of one type of communication situation from all the variables, one takes an element from each. An example for a highly homogeneous set of participants where communication effectiveness and efficiency are expected to be high would be as follows:

> Communication efficiency will be at the highest end of the continuum when direct channels are used by dyads of participants who perceive the relationship with the other as symmetrical, encompassing mutually positive feelings toward the other, and involving mutually shared and compatible goals; and the intent of the other is perceived as one of helping; having similar views of the nature of life, purpose of life and the relation of man to the cosmos; who know and accept the other's normative patterns of beliefs and overt behaviors; and who share a common code system.

The opposite end of the continuum is represented by the following statement:

> Communication efficiency will be at the lowest end of the continuum for participants when interposed channels are used by masses of parti-

cipants who perceive the relationship with the other as complementary, based on strongly negative feelings toward the other and with conflicting goals; who perceive the intent of the other to disrupt, dominate and injure them; who have very different views of the nature of life, purpose of life and relation of man to the cosmos; who do not know and if they did would not accept the normative patterns of beliefs and behaviors of the other; and where each knows a code system which is different from and unknown by the other.

The following pages will show the generation of the intermediate levels of homogeneity-heterogeneity and some intermediate stages of consolidating variables which contribute to varying levels of efficiency of communication.

The transitions from one level of homogeneity-heterogeneity to another is more apparent when a shorthand is used. The shorthand more concisely and visibly shows which changes are occurring in which of the variables from one level to another. The shorthand is the letters with number subscripts shown in parentheses after the labels for each of the variables on the following pages. The smaller the subscript, the more homogeneous; the larger the subscript, the more heterogeneous.

Within this chapter, the structure will be developed for one level of number of persons and one level of channel. Those will be dyads using direct channels. The levels of communication situations will then derive out of the various combinations of the other variables. That set of combinations could then be replicated for each of the channel types—direct and interposed—and for as many categories of number of persons as desired for each channel type and for the set of combinations of the other variables.

Before establishing the final structure, some initial combining will be done. This is intended to make the system more manageable and more meaningful. The first of these will combine the values of the variables *perceived relationship* (PR) and *intent* (I). The initial stage of that combining will be to establish three levels of intent—(a) sharing-helping (I_1); (b) ignoring (I_2); and (c) disrupting, dominating, or injuring (I_3). These three levels might be perceived as positive, neutral, and negative intent. In some cases, ignoring may represent a deliberate desire to communicate rejection of the other. That aspect of ignoring would be included under injuring in the present model.

The variable perceived relationship (PR) of the participants was described in Chapter 2 as having three dimensions:

a. A *feeling* (F) dimension ranging from strongly positive feelings toward one another (F_1) to strongly negative feelings toward one another (F_2).

b. A *goal* (G) dimension ranging from mutually shared and compatible goals which are cooperatively sought (G_1) to incompatible, conflicting, and competitive goals (G_2).

c. A *hierarchical* (H) dimension ranging from (H_1) least hierarchical, i.e., most nearly equal or symmetrical to (H_2) most strongly hierarchical, i.e., *complementary* or a strong superior-subordinate relationship.

If we take only the end values of those three dimensions and combine them, it yields eight combinations. If we further assume that $F_1G_1H_1$ is the most probable perceived relationship among homogeneous participants; and $F_2G_2H_2$ is most probable among highly heterogeneous participants, then four logical levels of perceived relationships are identifiable. They appear as follows:

	$F_1G_1H_1$		Level 1
$F_1G_1H_2$	$F_1G_2H_1$	$F_2G_1H_1$	Level 2
$F_1G_2H_2$	$F_2G_2H_1$	$F_2G_1H_2$	Level 3
	$F_2G_2H_2$		Level 4

At Level 1, all three dimensions are in the state associated with homogeneous participants who see themselves in a most positive feeling, cooperative, symmetrical state. At Level 2, we have the three combinations in which two of the three dimensions are in the state most conducive to sharing information, while one dimension (a different one in each case) is at the least conducive state for sharing information. At Level 3, one variable in each combination is at the most conducive state for sharing information while two are in the least conducive state for sharing information. At Level 4, all three are at the state considered least conducive for sharing information, i.e., $F_2G_2H_2$. It is a relationship of participants with strongly negative feelings toward one another; who have incompatible and conflicting goals; and who see themselves in a highly hierarchical relationship to one another.

You will recall that the claim was made that efficient communication involves moving from a state of independence to a state of interdependence. It is further claimed that an $F_1G_1H_1$ perceived relationship is most conducive to satisfactorily achieving the state of interdependence. $F_2G_2H_2$ then would be least conducive. The three combinations in each of the middle categories would appear to be on the same level within their category, as shown, unless there is some basis for weighting one of the dimensions as having more effect than the others. Lacking data for weighting, only the four levels will be shown here.

Intuitively, one might ask whether the combination of $F_2G_1H_1$ is likely to occur at all. Can persons who perceive strongly negative feelings toward one another at the same time perceive the relationship to be cooperative and symmetrical? It also is questionable whether persons can conceive of a participant in a transaction as being $F_2G_2H_1$. It may be difficult to imagine

Table 1—Combinations of *Perceived Relationships* and *Intent* of Participants

Levels of *Perceived Relationships* of Participants	INTENT OF PARTICIPANTS		
	Share-Help (I_1)	Ignoring (I_2)	Disrupt-Dominate-Injure (I_3)
$F_1G_1H_1$	$F_1G_1H_1\,I_1$ 1	Empty set 2	Empty set 3
$F_1G_1H_2$ $F_1G_2H_1$ $F_2G_1H_1$	$F_1G_1H_2\,I_1$ 4	Empty set 5	$F_1G_2H_1\,I_3$ $F_2G_1H_1\,I_3$ 6
$F_2G_1H_2$ $F_2G_2H_1$ $F_1G_2H_2$	$F_2G_1H_2I_1$ 7	$F_2G_1H_2\,I_2$ 8	$F_2G_1H_2\,I_3$ $F_2G_2H_1\,I_3$ $F_1G_2H_2\,I_3$ 9
$F_2G_2H_2$	Empty set 10	$F_2G_2H_2\,I_2$ 11	$F_2G_2H_2\,I_3$ 12

operating as an equal in that situation where there are conflicting goals and strongly negative feelings. The closest one might come to that condition would be in an exact balance of power situation, then there likely is a perception of the other trying to operate from a hierarchical perspective.

A MATRIX FOR INTENT AND PERCEIVED RELATIONSHIP

Earlier it was noted that a look at all the combinations of intent and perceived relationships would show some unlikely combinations. A matrix has been developed to show this. It uses the four levels of perceived relationship from the eight possible combinations of feeling (F_1)-(F_2), goals (G_1)-(G_2), and hierarchy (H_1)-(H_2), and three levels of intent (I_1, sharing and helping; I_2, ignoring; and I_3, disrupting-dominating-injuring).

Cell No. 3 in the top right corner of the matrix in Table 1 is shown as an empty set. The reasoning is that a relationship among participants that is perceived to be based on strongly positive feelings, mutually shared goals, and symmetrical ($F_1G_1H_1$) is antithetical to an intent of disrupting, dominating, or injuring (I_3). In Cells Nos. 2 and 5, an ignoring intent (I_2) also seems antithetical to a relationship that involves any two of the $F_1G_1H_1$ characteristics. In Cell No. 10 at the lower left corner of the matrix, a sharing-helping intent (I_1) seems antithetical to a superior-subordinate relationship with conflicting goals and negative feelings ($F_2G_2H_2$).

Cell No. 12 in the lower right corner of the matrix ($F_2G_2H_2\,I_3$) would seem to characterize those situations which involve fighting, war, and hard game playing.[1] Cell No. 7 described by $F_2G_1H_2\ I_1$ also may be one that is not often found, if at all. There may be some question as to the possibility of perceiving a person as being strongly negative toward me, mutual goals and complementary, and at the same time having an intent of sharing with or helping me.

The top left, Cell No. 1, and the lower right, Cell No. 12, of the matrix would represent the two ends of the continuum as far as positive-negative relationships and intent are concerned. The $F_1G_1H_1\ I_1$ combination would seem most likely to contribute to high efficiency of communication. The $F_2G_2H_2\ I_3$ combination would seem most likely to contribute to low efficiency of communication.

Since the main intent of this chapter is to share information about the components and form of the taxonomic system, further discussion of the relationship of these variables to other variables in the system will be delayed until specific cases are being discussed.

NORMATIVE PATTERNS OF BELIEFS AND OVERT BEHAVIORS

Values, role expectations, and other normative beliefs and overt behaviors, exclusive of world view, will be treated as one composite variable in the development of the taxonomy. Taken together, they express what one *must do, ought to do, is allowed to do, ought not do,* and *must not do.* "Do" in the present context is used to refer to both overt and covert behavior. There are injunctions about how one is expected to communicate as well as how one is expected to perform or not perform other behaviors. When the participants are homogeneous, they know and are controlled by the same set of injunctions. At the most heterogeneous level, the participants will neither know the injunctions of the other, nor would they accept and follow them if they were known.

A critical discriminator here will be the combination of knowing (K) and accepting and adhering to (A) the normative beliefs and overt behaviors of the other. There are 16 possible combinations of knowing (K) or not knowing ($\overline{K}$) and accepting (A) or not accepting ($\overline{A}$) for two persons or two groups of participants. However, six of these are reciprocal leaving 10 unduplicated combinations. In Table 2, all 16 combinations are shown and the duplicated combinations are indicated with an asterisk.

Note also that the thickness of the vertical lines by each set of knowing-accepting (KA) or not knowing-not accepting ($\overline{KA}$) is intended to indicate the relative intensity or extent of barriers to communication attributable to a particular combination. These social and psychological barriers are like walls and perhaps even more formidable than physical walls which people build to isolate themselves.

[1]Game playing here is in the sense used by Eric Berne, et al., under such labels as "uproar," "NigySOB," "Schlimiel," etc.

Table 2—Combinations of Knowing and Accepting in a Matrix of Behavioral Rules ("Must do"—"Must not do")

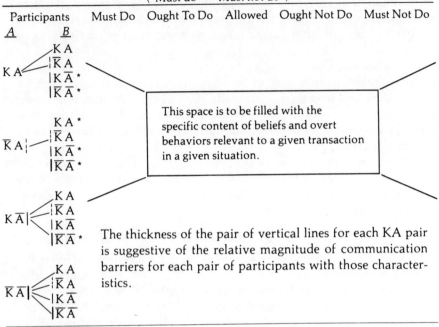

Participants		Must Do	Ought To Do	Allowed	Ought Not Do	Must Not Do
A	*B*					

This space is to be filled with the specific content of beliefs and overt behaviors relevant to a given transaction in a given situation.

The thickness of the pair of vertical lines for each KA pair is suggestive of the relative magnitude of communication barriers for each pair of participants with those characteristics.

*Indicates duplicated combinations

The combined thickness of the vertical lines is indicative of the magnitude of barriers to be overcome in a particular pairing of persons exhibiting each of the possible combinations of knowing-not knowing with accepting-not accepting. These are relative magnitudes, of course, and do not at this time represent any precisely measured magnitudes. The absence of lines between KA and KA suggests that this condition is as near to barrier free communication as can be achieved in respect to this set of variables.

To the right of the set of combinations from KA•KA to $\overline{KA}$•$\overline{KA}$ in Table 2, one can fill in the columns to check off *what* is known and *what* is accepted. This can be done for each level of injunction from *must do* to *must not do*. Such a matrix is a framework within which to specify the changes one would need to make in "knowing and/or accepting" to reduce heterogeneity and increase homogeneity of participants. It should point up the pathway to follow in increasing communication efficiency between the parties involved, i.e., tearing down walls. The highly obligatory "must do's" and highly taboo "must not do's" are the most critical behaviors to focus on in moving from a state of "not knowing" to "knowing" and from a condition of "not accepting" to one of at least tolerating, if not fully accepting the beliefs and overt behaviors of the other.

WORLD VIEW

Three dimensions of world view were discussed in Chapter 2—nature of life (NL), purpose of life (PL), and relation of man to the cosmos (RMC). If we assume that participants may differ on any one or all of these dimensions, there is a variety of combinations which are possible. If we again take the extremes of similar-dissimilar for each of the three dimensions, there are eight possible combinations of world view represented. These fall into four levels of similarity-dissimilarity, as follows:

	$NL_1PL_1RMC_1$		Level 1
$NL_1PL_1RMC_2$	$NL_1PL_2RMC_1$	$NL_2PL_1RMC_1$	Level 2
$NL_1PL_2RMC_2$	$NL_2PL_1RMC_2$	$NL_2PL_2RMC_1$	Level 3
	$NL_2PL_2RMC_2$		Level 4

Level 1 includes persons who are similar on all three dimensions. This can be expressed as $NL_1PL_1RMC_1$, with the subscript 1 indicating high similarity for all three dimensions. In the subsequent levels, the subscript 2 indicates high dissimilarity.

Level 2 includes persons who differ on only one of the dimensions of world view. Level 3 includes persons who differ on two of the three dimensions. Level 4 includes persons who differ greatly on all three dimensions; it is, of course, the most dissimilar.

As with perceived relationships of the participants, we can establish four levels of homogeneity-heterogeneity, given the assumption of equal weighting of the dimensions, and the assumption that subscript 1 values are more homogeneous than subscript 2 values for each dimension. Note from Chapter 2, there are several levels of similarity-dissimilarity of codes, as there are for each of the variables. These will not be repeated here.

THE STRUCTURE OF THE TAXONOMY

In the preceding pages, some of the variables have been consolidated to achieve a more manageable form for the taxonomy. As stated earlier, the portion of the taxonomy presented here will be for dyads using direct channels. Four other sets of variables developed by the intermediate combining operations, will be used to describe 36 sets of situations which will be rank ordered from most homogeneous to most heterogeneous, given the assumptions noted in earlier pages. Those four sets of variables are: (1) perceived relationship and intent of participants (PRI); (2) code system (CS); (3) level of knowing and accepting of normative patterns of beliefs and overt behaviors (KA); and (4) world view (WV).

The polar ends of the continuum will be used for all four sets of variables, with the addition of a middle level for code system (CS) and for knowing-accepting (KA). This is done for two basic reasons, first to gain parsimony, and second it is doubtful that the sophistication of measurement at this stage will permit detection of fine degrees of discrimination. If the system has utility when using only the ends of the continuums, then adding levels later should improve the precision and utility. Table 3 shows the way the four sets of variables are combined to generate the taxonomic sets and levels of Table 4.

The first of the four sets of variables in Table 3 is perceived relationship and perceived intent (PRI). The two ends of the continuum are represented by Cells No. 1 and No. 12 in Table 1. These are $F_1G_1H_1I_1$ which will be shown in Table 3 as PRI_1. Translated from the shorthand, that is a relationship which is perceived as symmetrical, not hierarchical (H_1), with strongly positive feeling for one another (F_1), mutually shared and compatible goals for which they are striving together, sometimes referred to as a cooperative or promotive relationship (G_1), and with the intent of sharing and helping one another (I_1).

PRI_2, the other end of the perceived relationship and intent variable ($F_2G_2H_2I_2$), may be translated out of the shorthand as follows: The relationship is perceived as being highly hierarchical (H_2), with strongly negative feelings for one another (F_2), incompatible and antagonistic or conflicting goals (G_2), and with an intent to dominate, disrupt, and injure (I_3) one another.

The second variable set, code system (CS), will include three levels of homogeneity-heterogeneity. The most homogeneous is CS_1 in which both participants share the same code system. CS_2 is an intermediate level in which the participants share a common code, but one or both may have an additional code system which is not shared by the other. The most heterogeneous situation CS_3, is where the participants do not have a common code system which they can use in an attempted transaction.

The third variable set is levels of knowing and accepting of the normative patterns of beliefs and overt behaviors. Three levels will be used with KA_1 being most homogeneous, KA_2 being an intermediate level, and KA_3 being the most heterogeneous. The chart below will show the composition of the three levels covering the 10 unduplicated combinations noted in Table 2:

KA_1	KA_2	KA_3
$KA \cdot KA$	$\overline{KA} \cdot KA$	$\overline{KA} \cdot KA$
$KA \cdot \overline{KA}$	$\overline{KA} \cdot \overline{KA}$	$\overline{KA} \cdot \overline{KA}$
$\overline{KA} \cdot \overline{KA}$	$\overline{KA} \cdot \overline{KA}$	$\overline{KA} \cdot \overline{KA}$
		$\overline{KA} \cdot \overline{KA}$

The fourth variable set is that of world view (WV). It will be included at only the two end levels, WV_1 as most homogeneous and WV_2 as most heterogeneous. WV_1 indicates those participants who are very much alike on their views of the nature of life (NL_1), the purpose of life (PL_1) and the relation of man to the cosmos (RMC_1). WV_2 indicates those participants who are very different in their views on those three dimensions as represented in the shorthand by $NL_2PL_2RMC_2$.

Table 3 shows the values of the four sets of variables and the connecting lines suggest the combinations. It will produce 36 combinations of the variables for the one set of conditions pertaining to number of persons and channel, i.e., for dyads using direct channels. These are listed in Table 4. The shorthand used in Table 4 is the letter and number subscript combinations shown in Table 3.

The connecting lines in Table 3 can be followed from the left to the right of the page to generate each of the 36 combinations which appear in Table 4. For example, the lines across the top of the page connecting PRI_1 to CS_1 to KA_1 to WV_1 is set No. 1 in the taxonomy shown in Table 4; it is the combination claimed to describe the most homogeneous participants in communication events.

If you follow the lines across the bottom of the page, connecting PRI_2 to CS_3 to KA_3 to WV_2, you get the description of the most heterogeneous participants. That combination appears as set No. 36 in the taxonomy shown in Table 4.

The connecting lines in Table 3 first show the three combinations of PRI_1 with each of the three levels code system (CS_1, CS_2, and CS_3). The same can be done with PRI_2 to create three more combinations. Now each of those six pairs can be connected with each of the three levels of KA (KA_1, KA_2, and KA_3) to produce 18 combinations. Each of these sets of 18 can now be combined with the two levels of WV (WV_1 and WV_2) to produce the 36 combinations. Mathematically it is two levels of PRI multiplied by three levels of CS multiplied by three levels of KA multiplied by two levels of WV ($2 \times 3 \times 3 \times 2 = 36$).

As shown in Table 3, this is only for dyads using direct channels. The same 36 combinations could be attached to interposed channels to produce 36 additional combinations or a total of 72 combinations when two categories of the channel variable are included. This process of selecting a given number of levels, or categories, for each of the variables, then generating all the possible combinations of those categories of the variables[2] produced the taxonomy in Table 4.

The attempt is made with the taxonomy to show the ordering from most homogeneous to most heterogeneous. As you look at the order, you

[2]Appendix A contains a list of all the shorthand codes used to label the elements within each of the sets of variables.

Table 3—Values of Variables Used to Form Combined Categories

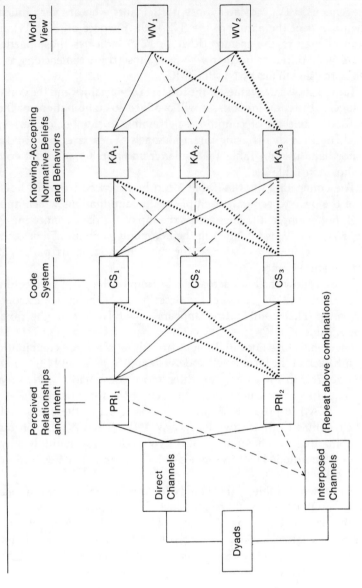

Table 4—Taxonomic Categories for Homogeneity-Heterogeneity of Participants in Transactions

Set No.	Perceived Relation and Intent	Code System	Knowing-Accepting of Normative Beliefs and Behaviors	World View	Sum of Subscripts	Level
1.	PRI_1	CS_1	KA_1	WV_1	4	1
2.	PRI_2	CS_1	KA_1	WV_1	5	
3.	PRI_1	CS_2	KA_1	WV_1	5	
4.	PRI_1	CS_1	KA_2	WV_1	5	2
5.	PRI_1	CS_1	KA_1	WV_2	5	
6.	PRI_1	CS_3	KA_1	WV_1	6	
7.	PRI_2	CS_2	KA_1	WV_1	6	
8.	PRI_2	CS_1	KA_2	WV_1	6	
9.	PRI_2	CS_1	KA_1	WV_2	6	3
10.	PRI_1	CS_2	KA_2	WV_1	6	
11.	PRI_1	CS_2	KA_1	WV_2	6	
12.	PRI_1	CS_1	KA_2	WV_2	6	
13.	PRI_1	CS_1	KA_3	WV_1	6	
14.	PRI_2	CS_3	KA_1	WV_1	7	
15.	PRI_2	CS_2	KA_2	WV_1	7	
16.	PRI_2	CS_2	KA_1	WV_2	7	
17.	PRI_2	CS_1	KA_2	WV_2	7	
18.	PRI_1	CS_2	KA_2	WV_2	7	4
19.	PRI_1	CS_3	KA_2	WV_1	7	
20.	PRI_1	CS_3	KA_1	WV_2	7	
21.	PRI_2	CS_1	KA_3	WV_1	7	
22.	PRI_1	CS_2	KA_3	WV_1	7	
23.	PRI_1	CS_1	KA_3	WV_2	7	
24.	PRI_2	CS_3	KA_2	WV_1	8	
25.	PRI_2	CS_3	KA_1	WV_2	8	
26.	PRI_1	CS_3	KA_2	WV_2	8	
27.	PRI_2	CS_2	KA_2	WV_2	8	
28.	PRI_2	CS_2	KA_3	WV_1	8	5
29.	PRI_1	CS_3	KA_3	WV_1	8	
30.	PRI_2	CS_1	KA_3	WV_2	8	
31.	PRI_1	CS_2	KA_3	WV_2	8	
32.	PRI_2	CS_3	KA_3	WV_1	9	
33.	PRI_2	CS_3	KA_2	WV_2	9	
34.	PRI_1	CS_3	KA_3	WV_2	9	6
35.	PRI_2	CS_2	KA_3	WV_2	9	
36.	PRI_2	CS_3	KA_3	WV_2	10	7

Various Combinations of Number of Persons and Channels May Be Attached to Each Category

very likely may have a different opinion as to the ordering of some of the categories. I believe the challenge to all of us should be to empirically demonstrate the appropriate ordering of communication events along a continuum from homogeneous (intracultural) to heterogeneous (intercultural). As already noted, the basic assumption is that as interculturalness increases, the efficiency of communication will decline.

The sets in Table 4 will be numbered beginning with the most homogeneous as No. 1 to the most heterogeneous as No. 36. The sets were written in the shorthand in Table 3 both to conserve space and to increase the visibility of the change in values of the variables for each item. Table 3 showed all the elements which were combined. Remember that in the shorthand in Tables 3 and 4 a subscript of 1 implies similarity, a subscript of 2 implies dissimilarity; and a subscript of 3 implies still greater dissimilarity; i.e., the larger the subscript in the designation of a value of a variable the greater the heterogeneity.

LEVELS OF INTERCULTURALNESS

With this systematic pattern of combining variables, seven levels of interculturalness are identified from the 36 combinations. If there were some known way of weighting each of the variables, greater accuracy in designating levels could be achieved. In arriving at the ordering within each of the levels, stability of the characteristic and presumed resistance to change were considered. It was assumed that from least to most resistance would be $PRI < CS < KA < WV$. Thus the suggestion is that a difference in world view would be more resistant to change and more difficult to move from heterogeneous to homogeneous than would a difference in code systems between the participants.

The first combination shown is clearly the most homogeneous. It matches the description at the beginning of this chapter for a highly homogeneous set. The last item shown, item 36, is clearly the most heterogeneous, given that equal weighting of the variables is assumed. It differs from the description of the heterogeneous set at the beginning of the chapter only in channel and number of persons. The first has a 1 as the subscript for each variable; the last has a 3 for two variables and a 2 as a subscript for each of the other variables, thus indicating the greatest diversity. Adding the subscripts for the values of the variables provides a guide to ordering the shorthand descriptions of situations generated in Table 4.

The lowest sum is 4 for the most homogeneous situation; the highest sum is 10 for the most heterogeneous situation.

It may be noted that as we move from Level 1 to Level 2, one variable has been shifted to the heterogeneous end of the continuum, alternating among the variables for each set at that level. When we move from Level 2 to Level 3, two variables instead of one are moved toward the heterogeneous end of the continuum for all but sets No. 6 and No. 13; and so on through each level until all variables are at the most heterogeneous end of the continuum in set No. 36.

Data are lacking as to the relative impact on communication outcomes that would result from a shift in homogeneity-heterogeneity of any one of the variables. Thus there is not a good rationale for ordering the sets within levels. One basis for the ordering within each level is the presumed stability and resistance to change of each of the characteristics of people represented by the variables. You will remember that in Chapter 2 perceived relationship and intent were discussed as the variables most susceptible to change; world view was considered the most stable and resistant to change. While it has been pointed out that definitive data are not available to establish a weighting of the variables, the reasoning just presented has been used to the extent possible, in the ordering within levels.

Items 2 through 5 each contain one variable with a subscript of 2. Unless there are some data to indicate that one variable is more critical than another in the communication process, there is no logical way of claiming that one of these four combinations is any more heterogeneous than the others. Thus, in the application examples all sets in a given Level will be assumed to be approximately equivalent in heterogeneity.

To help with the interpretation of the sets of situations, I will describe a situation that would correspond to set No. 6 ($PRI_1CS_3KA_1WV_1$) under Level 3. The description would read:

> This is a relatively homogeneous situation in which the participants see their relationship to one another involving strongly positive feelings, mutually shared and compatible goals, and being symmetrical rather hierarchical. They see their intent toward one another as one of sharing and helping. They do not share a common code system and that appears to be the main barrier to efficient transactions between them. Both of them know and accept the normative patterns of beliefs and overt behaviors of the other; and they have similar views of the nature of life, purpose of life and of the relation of man to the cosmos.

Hopefully this example will illustrate how a description can be derived from the taxonomy. The reverse operation also may be used. A narrative description may be converted into one of the taxonomic categories. That should help one assess the potential level of difficulty one is likely to experience with a given situation.

Sets 7 through 12 each contain two variables with subscripts of 2. Sets 6 and 13 are distinctive in the ordering for sums of 6; each has one subscript of 3 and three variables with subscripts of 1. Logically, sets Nos. 6–13 should be more heterogeneous than any of the first five combinations (sets Nos. 1–5).

There is no logical basis, however, for claiming that any one of the eight combinations in Level 3 is more hetereogeneous than any of the other seven
combinations in sets 6 to 13.

A description of another of the sets in Table 4 may help you understand
the operation of the taxonomy a little more fully and some of its potential.
A description for set No. 17 ($PRI_2CS_1KA_2WV_2$) would read:

> The situation is moderately high on the heterogeneity scale. The par-
> ticipants perceive their relationship with one another as involving
> strongly negative feelings toward one another, incompatible and con-
> flicting goals, and as being strongly hierarchical. They see their intent
> toward one another as one of dominating and possibly injuring the
> other. If they don't already know it, they will find that one or both of
> them does not accept the normative patterns of beliefs and overt be-
> haviors of the other. They also hold dissimilar views on the nature of
> life, purpose of life and the relation of man to the cosmos. They do
> share a common code. However, with the differences on the other
> dimensions, one would suspect that somewhat different meanings
> would be elicited by the same symbols in the same context. The simi-
> larity of the code system does provide them a starting point if they
> have the desire to establish interdependent activity. They may discover
> that the differences in beliefs offer an exciting complement to their own
> beliefs. The major initial problem to overcome would seem to be the
> negativeness of the perceived relationship and intent.

It could be argued that communication would be easier and more
efficient in set No. 18 than in set No. 17 which was just described. Set No. 18
starts with a positive perceived relationship and intent (PRI_1) and they share
one common code while one of them has a second code (CS_2), and they are
at the same level of heterogeneity on the other two variables (KA_2 and WV_2).
The differences in beliefs may affect the meanings elicited by the same
symbols; thus, there is some uncertainty as to which of these two sets would
result in more efficient communication with present knowledge of the
operation of these variables.

Somewhat more certainty exists if the comparison is between set No. 11
which is in Level 3 of the taxonomy and either set No. 17 or set No. 18 both
of which are in Level 4 of the taxonomy. The homogeneity of beliefs (KA_1)
and the perceived positive relationship (PRI_1) of set No. 11 would lead to
the prediction of more open communication and more shared meanings
than for either set No. 17 or No. 18.

These examples should indicate some of the potential uses of the
taxonomy; and suggest the need for more data on the way the different
combinations of the variables affect communication outcomes. Those data

can come from empirical study and analysis of communication events at different levels of homogeneity-heterogeneity as defined by the taxonomic categories. It would seem most appropriate at first to compare categories from nonadjacent levels so as to build in greater presumed differences of homogeneity-heterogeneity. Work could then proceed to comparing categories which are closer together in the taxonomy, i.e., less difference in homogeneity-heterogeneity.

The combining of the four sets of variables, using extreme values, and adding an intermediate value for two of the variables, yields the taxonomy containing the 36 combinations of the variables to describe 36 different types of communication situations. Given those 36 combinations, and the assumptions for homogeneity-heterogeneity, the seven levels of interculturalness can be posited.

If 10 combinations of number of persons and channels (5 number of persons sets × 2 channels) were added to the variables in building arrays of combinations, the number of combinations would be increased to 360 (10 × 36). It has been claimed in this text that the number of persons and channels does not establish the interculturalness of the situation; it is claimed, however, that they do increase the complexity of the communication as the number of persons increases and as interposed rather than direct channels are used. It also has been noted that under some conditions, interposed channels may actually facilitate the communication.

It should be apparent that many, many more combinations are possible if additional values were used for each of the variables, values which are intermediate between the polar ends of the continuum which were used in Table 4. This would provide a greater variety of situations than have been presented here.

I believe there is a general awareness that intercultural communication is complex and generally highly unpredictable relative to intracultural communication. It seems that the systematic listing of different combinations of the main variables operating in communication dramatizes that complexity.

The taxonomy suggests several questions which those involved in intercultural communication should ask:

1. For which of the variables does dissimilarity have the least impact on the outcome of the communication?
2. For which, if any, of the variables is dissimilarity a barrier to communication only when combined with dissimilarity in one or more of the other variables?
3. For which of the variables can dissimilarity be most easily compensated for with a third party intermediary?
4. For which, if any, of the variables is it impossible to compensate for dissimilarity by using a third party as intermediary?

To those questions may be added several others regarding ways of reducing dissimilarity and/or adapting to it in the several types of intercultural situations.

Research, to this point, has not looked at the operation of the variables in terms of levels of interculturalness; so, the available data are not organized in this manner. A high priority task could be the synthesizing of the various pieces of research under this kind of systematic framework.

EXERCISES

1. Write the taxonomic description for two communication situations in which you engaged during the past week:
   a. One which was highly satisfying and which you judged highly efficient.
   b. One which was not satisfying and which you judged not effective or efficient.
2. If you were to add variables to those used in the taxonomy, what would you add and why?
3. If you were to delete variables from the taxonomy, what would you delete and why?
4. If you were to combine variables still further or in a different way, what would you combine?

4

Principles of Communication
Applied Interculturally

A goal of scholarship is to generate generalizations which apply beyond the specific situation in which a set of relationships is observed. In the writing on intercultural communication, there have been numerous inventories of anecdotal reports and inferences drawn from them. These are useful and important guides to behavior for anyone involved in intercultural communication, and that is most of us in some degree.

The goal here is to develop a systematic set of generalizations which may be used to derive testable hypotheses in research, and as principles to guide communication practice both in predicting outcomes and in explaining those outcomes experienced. The taxonomic scheme presented in Chapter 3 and the categories of situations generated from it are intended to provide a base from which to develop generalizations that will apply to sets of those situations.

The generalizations will be stated both in terms of (1) correlational statements, i.e., as A increases, B will increase (or decrease) proportionately; and (2) implied causality, i.e., if A occurs, then B follows; A is the antecedent condition which always precedes the outcome (or consequence) B.

The generalizations will be grouped according to the variables used in the preceding chapters. Some of these will be found to apply at all levels of interculturalness in communication. In every case, the increase in heterogeneity of participants is believed to intensify the effect of the variables in reducing efficiency of communication. That leads to the first principle which is a broad one applying to intercultural communication generally.

> **Principle #1**—As the heterogeneity of the participants in a communication situation increases, the efficiency of the communication will decline.

As noted earlier, efficiency is the resultant of the extent to which participants achieve desired outcomes in relation·to energy input.

PRINCIPLES PERTAINING TO NUMBER OF PARTICIPANTS

Principle #2—As the number of persons participating in a communication increases, the number of potential alternate outcomes increases.

This principle derives from the notion that each person potentially has some unique elements to add to the situation. As the number of these elements increases, the number of possible combinations of elements increases. With the generation of new combinations of elements, the potential for new alternatives will increase. Up to a point, this is likely to improve the quality of solutions to problems and produce increasingly satisfying outcomes. At some point, which I cannot specify, the burden of deciding among an increased set of alternatives becomes so overpowering as to interfere with effective communication. It may reach a point of such frustration that withdrawal or aggression is used to cope.

Principle #3—As the number of participants increases, the time and energy required to achieve consensus of an issue or question requiring resolution, will increase at an increasing rate.

This phenomenon is readily demonstrated by having persons individually write solutions to a problem, then subsequently in groups of varying sizes find a solution that all will agree to. An easy exercise in which to have people experience this is to have them rank order some set of items in terms of their importance in a given situation. That set of items could be: the most important elements in communication, or national leaders who contribute most to peace in our world, or any other set of relevant items. Then have two persons seek consensus on their respective rankings. Next have four persons seek a common ranking, then eight persons. The point likely will be established by this time.

As the heterogeneity of participants increases, the diversity of assumptions with which a situation is approached will increase. That diversity will add to the time and energy required to reach agreement for each size group.

Principle #4—As the number of participants increases, the possibility of direct channel participation will decline with a concommitant increase in the number of passive persons in the situation.

Principle #5—As the number of persons participating in a communication event increases, the need for interposed channels increases.

Principle #6—When an individual has others with him who hold to a similar view, he is more likely to express that view and cling to it in the face of opposing views.

In principle #4, let's take the example of trying to speak to a large number of persons. The possibility of being heard becomes increasingly difficult as the size of the crowd forces listeners farther away from the speaker. Furthermore, the possibility of directing the communication to deal with the interests of the different persons becomes less and less possible as the number of persons increases. As either of the preceding situations occurs, passivity or restlessness will increase. The need to overcome the physical distance among participants leads to principle #5.

Principle #6 is the "social pressure/social support" principle. It operates most effectively in a direct channel situation where relatively small numbers are involved; however, it also operates with interposed channels. This is evident in the bandwagon effect that occurs during political campaigns or other comparable conditions.

The mass media make it possible to learn about others who share similar views with which I may identify. That knowledge of others sharing my viewpoint can encourage me to speak out for the view I hold. This encouragement may be most important to me when I'm faced with persons whose views and beliefs are appreciably different, i.e., the intercultural situation.

Principle #6 would say that it is very helpful to have others of my own culture with me when I'm communicating interculturally. The social support can add immeasurably to my comfort and encourage me to continue the communication effort. If we accept the notion that fear and anxiety interfere with effective communication, then the social support could serve to reduce the fear and anxiety and permit more effective communication. There also is a danger lurking in principle #6 if the intent is to bridge intercultural gaps. The social support from available homogeneous others may reduce the desire to engage in transactions with heterogeneous others. It also may serve to intensify the ingroup beliefs and impede the desire or willingness to learn about the beliefs and behaviors of the heterogeneous others. Consistently pursued, such a pattern of restricting communication flow will restrict one's knowledge of the universe.

CHANNEL PRINCIPLES

Principle #7—If a direct channel is used instead of an interposed channel, the immediacy of feedback, the availability of more sensory cues, and access to a fuller social context will result in more effective communication.

Any interposed person or mechanical device limits certain aspects of the experience for those engaged in the transaction. While there may be more effective communication with a direct channel, a direct channel may be impossible to use due to physical separation. Interposed channels make possible the bridging of time and distance.

Access to additional context and additional sensory cues is nearly always helpful; it is especially important, even necessary, in intercultural communication where additional reference points are needed to validate one's interpretation of the codes received. The immediacy also is greatly needed in intercultural transactions to permit checking one's interpretations of messages.

As noted earlier, some interposed channels now offer two-way immediate transmission. This is the case with telephone and with two-way cable television. This situation would help offset limits suggested above for interposed channels. The limitation on available sensory cues and context would still hold, however.

Principle #8—If the interposed channel is a person rather than a mechanical device, then greater variability in the transmission will occur.

With a properly functioning mechanical device, the code produced by the communicator is received in the same form by the communicator on the receiving end of the transaction. The decoding may not be what the source intended, but the code elements were the same at the input and output ends. As implied in principle #1, the probability of misinterpretation increases with heterogeneity of the participants. Nevertheless, the code has been relayed as produced by the source.

When a person is the interposed element, the code delivered to the receiver also is likely to be different. The person is not an inactive transmitter. The interposed person receives the code from the source, decodes it into meaningful thought; then encodes it and transmits it to the intended receiver. In that process, the fidelity is expected to be relatively high when all the persons involved are highly homogeneous. When they are heterogeneous, the interposed channel (person) may serve a clarifying function or may add to distortion of the message. The serial transmission (rumor clinic) phenomenon, where a stimulus is observed by one person, then relayed to another, who then relays it to another, and so on, is a dramatic illustration of the variations in messages which may develop with persons as interposed channels.

In the intercultural communication situation, the importance of the interposed person knowing and understanding both cultures should be apparent from this discussion. In that situation, the interposed person can serve a clarifying function. If that person does not know both cultures and the relation of the topic to those cultures, then the clarifying function is greatly reduced, even lost, or may increase a confusion. That's the range of variability stated in principle #8.

Principle #9—Given that distortion tends to increase with each additional link in the communication chain, the increase in distortion will be accentuated when the communication is intercultural.

This principle seems fairly evident following the reference to the serial transmission phenomenon under principle #8. If we accept that communication effectiveness tends to be lower among heterogeneous (intercultural) participants than among homogeneous participants (intracultural) then each additional link in the chain would be expected to magnify the distortions at each succeeding stage.

The limiting factors with interposed channels, noted in principle #7, also would contribute to the message deterioration. Misinterpretations are present in communication even under the most favorable conditions. To minimize the misinterpretations, it is accepted practice to use multiple channels and immediate feedback to the fullest extent practical. With increases in the probability of misinterpretation, as in the case of intercultural situations, it becomes even more urgent to use multiple channels and immediate feedback.

> **Principle #10**—If an interposed channel is used, then the credence given to the message will be in proportion to the credibility of the interposed channel.

In many situations there are both people and mechanical devices interposed between a communication event and the person who is receiving and responding to the report of that event. This is always the case with a story which appears in a newspaper. The news reporter observes the event and writes about it; an editor modifies it; it is then set in type, printed, and distributed. Credence given to the report will depend on the prior experience of the receiver with that particular newspaper. If the newspaper (interposed channel) has a reputation for accuracy of reporting and printing for the particular receiver, then the receiver will give high credence to the report.

In any interposed channel situation, the person handling the input and output of the channel engages in a selection and encoding process. Critical judgments are involved in that process, and receivers over time are able to decide how complete and accurate the selection and encoding has been.

One of the dilemmas of dealing with interposed channels is that many times a receiver has no way of confirming or disconfirming the messages received. It then becomes very confusing when conflicting reports of the "same" event are received. The extent to which that situation is exacerbated in intercultural communication will be stressed in the later principles dealing with heterogeneity of participants.

There are some situations in which an interposed channel will be preferred. Among these are situations in which the participants experience intense emotional pressures in a direct channel confrontation. I've seen cases of this where a person did not wish to face another person with an apology for some act; or where the pain of saying farewell face-to-face seemed to be too great. It is generally a case where feelings, either positive or negative, are extremely strong.

> **Principle #11**—If the communication is one which may involve intense stress or uncertainty, then an interposed channel may be preferred by the participants and result in more effective communication.

One of the advantages of the interposed channel in such a situation is that more time may be used for careful construction of the message. One may even seek help in constructing the message without this being apparent to the receiver. This principle serves to point out that special conditions exist in which exceptions will be found to the most general principle. Here it is noted that while direct channels generally provide for higher fidelity and effectiveness of communication, there are some situations in which that is not the case.

PRINCIPLES RE: PERCEIVED RELATIONSHIPS AND INTENT

Principle #12—(a) If the relationship is perceived as friendly, cooperative, and symmetrical and the intent is one of sharing and helping (PRI_1), then information will be shared among the participants.

(b) Conversely, if the relationship is perceived as hostile, competitive, and complementary and the intent is to dominate, disrupt, or injure (PRI_2), then information will be hoarded by the participants.

In the model presented here, principle #12-a specifies the condition which is at the homogeneous end of the continuum, and #12-b specifies the condition at the heterogeneous end of the continuum. Thus, the claim is made that sharing of information will be more likely to occur and with fewer reservations in intracultural situations than in intercultural situations. The level of trust is higher among participants with strongly positive feelings toward one another and who perceive themselves in a cooperative relationship among equals. In a situation where there is perceived hostility, competitiveness and a strong superior-subordinate relationship, there will be distrust of the other.

In the hostile, competitive, symmetrical, dominating relationship and intent, the situation tends to get defined as "I win, you lose; you win, I lose." Rather than mutually shared goals, the goals are conflicting. This will lead to restricting message flow and even to transmitting messages intended to deceive. Often when interpersonal relationships get defined as "I win, you lose; you win, I lose" both parties choose communication strategies which lead to both losing. They lose some of the benefits that would be available if they were to combine their energies toward a common goal.

In a community action program to solve a transportation problem, for example, opposing groups may hold out for their own method of solving the problem. The outcome may well be that nothing is done to solve the problem and both groups suffer the consequences of inadequate transportation. The larger goal of improved transportation gets lost in the struggle by each group to achieve the adoption of *their own* plan. Much energy has been expended with the main outcome being increased frustration, while the transportation problem becomes more serious.

In an office, a similar situation may arise where two persons are seeking the same position and only one can have it. Hoarding of information may be used by each person as a way of gaining advantage and may carry beyond the decision to select one of the persons for the position. Such relationships can be disastrous in achieving the task goals of the office, unless the r _rsons can commit themselves to a larger goal of efficient and effective operation of the office.

Other illustrations of the "I win, you lose; you win, I lose" condition would be: (1) athletic teams exerting great effort to keep their practice sessions secret; or (2) business firms conducting market surveys and exercising numerous precautions to keep their findings from a competitor. There may even be efforts to plant misinformation to deceive the other. The use of misinformation perhaps reaches the highest state of development in wartime, where each side develops specialists in deception.

At the other end of the scale where if one wins the other(s) also wins, examples would include members of the same athletic team; members of the same business firm or the same unit in the firm; husband, wife, and children with shared family goals; or members of a group seeking to complete a community improvement project. In the business firm, the breakthrough for a new product requires sharing information among the engineering, design, market research, production, and distribution units. If each is successful, then all are successful; if anyone fails, then all fail in achieving the final outcome. Here secrecy or deception among the units would be detrimental to all.

The hierarchical (symmetrical-complementary) variable may be less critical than others in relation to principle #12. However, there is evidence in the group and organizational literature (e.g., Blau and Scott, 1962) which demonstrates that where there is a recognized status difference between communicators, communication will be less free and open than when there is a perception of approximately equal status.

If one party in the intercultural transaction feels inferior and the other feels superior, the stage is set for the complementary component of the perceived relationship. This often is the case with a person from a minority culture talking with a person from the majority culture. This likely will result in the tendency to withhold information rather than full sharing.

When persons or groups of two different cultures are engaging in a transaction, there may be more uncertainty as to the perceived relationship and intent. With the uncertainty there is likely to be more caution about sharing information. It will influence not only what things are communicated about, but in what depth and detail. This is reflected in the safe, superficial topics about which two strangers will talk—weather, number in family, etc.

There also is the condition in which I feel that the outcome for the other has no implications for my well-being. In that case, I may be quite free to share information; but I would not feel the obligation to share as I would in the situation where the outcome for the other directly affects what happens to me.

Principle #13—As the perceived intent of the communicators shifts from sharing-helping (I_1), to disrupting-dominating-injuring (I_3), there will be an increase in deliberate efforts to distort and deceive in the messages transmitted.

References to cases where this might occur already have been presented in the discussion following principle #12. It represents the shift from a climate of trust to distrust; a shift from interdependent activity with a shared goal to activity designed to control, embarrass, or overpower the other.

Principle #14—As the perceived relationship and intent moves from most homogeneous (PRI_1) to most heterogeneous (PRI_2), the probability of communication breakdown increases.

Principles #12 and #13 culminate in this principle. Communication breakdown is increased when restrictions are set on dissemination of information; and breakdown is virtually assured when deliberate distortion and deception are injected into a transaction. The PRI_2 participants are likely to be so obsessed with establishing dominance that the content of the message becomes lost in the relationship battle.

In the literature on interpersonal communication there is the statement that "hostility begets hostility." That leads to what Berne labels a game of uproar. In this game each participant is critical of the other in a put-down sense. If the other would respond in a submissive way, then communication could proceed with attention to content rather than focusing solely on relationship. However, when both participants are desiring the other to be submissive, a shouting match is likely to ensue and the topic of communication (outside the relationship issue) becomes lost in the uproar.

In the intercultural situation, there may be a feeling of cultural superiority for "own" culture by each of the participants. Or there may be negative feelings toward and suspicion of the outsider. The fear and anxiety which may accompany the uncertainty about the other culture may result in defensiveness with tendencies of negative feelings toward the other, either subtle or more open and explicit.

PRINCIPLES RELATED TO CODE SYSTEMS

Principle #15—If the participants do not share a common code system (both verbal and nonverbal) or have a mechanism for translating into a common code, then the desired communication becomes impossible.[1]

A common code which both share or which some third party can provide is a necessary, but not sufficient, condition for effective communication. Many cases of communication breakdown occur around us daily where the participants speak the "same" language but fail to elicit the intended meaning in the other. This emphasizes the oft repeated statement that meanings are in people, not in symbols. It is only to the extent that we both have shared common experiences in association with a symbol that it will elicit similar meanings for both of us. It's this sort of thing that can be handled with the present model in classifying intra- and intercultural communication and predicting more accurately the situations in which communication difficulties are likely to occur.

As noted in Chapter 2, there are differing levels of sharing or having unique code systems. As noted above, there is the situation where two persons have the same words, but they have not had the same or even similar experiences in association with those words. It is also possible that two persons or groups have different words but have had similar experiences and merely label them differently. They also could have different experiences in relation to certain objects or relationships between persons and have different labels to denote those experiences.

It seems fairly obvious that the third party serving as interpreter (translator) has a relatively easy task when the experiences are similar but the labels for those experiences are different. Two teachers among the so-called Western cultures may have relatively similar patterns of teaching, but different labels. Here, the translator can be very useful; and with simultaneous translation, the communication can proceed at a relatively standard rate and minimum risk of breakdown.

One level noted in the levels of code systems (pp. 35–36) was that in which one person knows two codes and the other knows only one of the two. An example of this would be an inner city black in the U.S.A. who knows the black dialect and "standard" English while the other participant is a suburban white who knows only "standard" English. It seems fairly

---

[1]There is a point of view which says that you cannot "not communicate." When the participants do not share a common code, there is a message which the participants can both decode; namely, that they can't communicate as they wish.

obvious that this situation will present some communication difficulties not experienced in transactions by two suburban whites or two inner city blacks.

Even when the black and the white referred to above are in a transaction using "standard" English, the set of experiences differs, and the denotations and connotations for the codes are more likely to vary for them. The black has the advantage of being both bilingual and bicultural, assuming that "standard" English was learned in situations where there were participants who lived outside the inner city.

PRINCIPLES RELATED TO KNOWING AND ACCEPTING WORLD VIEW, VALUES, ROLE EXPECTATIONS, AND OTHER NORMATIVE BELIEFS AND BEHAVIORS

Principle #16—(a) If two participants in a communication have different patterns of beliefs and behaviors, then they will have different assumptions from which they will respond to stimuli.

(b) As two participants approach a communication transaction with different assumptions, the perceptions of the stimuli and the meanings elicited by them will differ.

The variables contained in principle #16 are the most central to the determination of homogeneity-heterogeneity of participants. They deal with fundamental belief systems. Our assumptions are formed out of our beliefs; hence, as those beliefs differ, our assumptions differ.

Among the major impediments to effective communication are a lack of awareness of the assumptions one is making in drawing inferences, and confusing inferences with fact. This is noted repeatedly in contemporary materials on communication. Haney (1967) with his critical inference tests brought this into focus several years ago; and tests to help one identify inferences and assumptions abound in communication training programs.

It is not unusual to find persons in heated argument operating from two different sets of assumptions and not aware of the assumptions either is making. When the assumptions of both are made explicit, the conclusions being drawn by each then appear reasonable, given the assumptions.

Using the definition of increased interculturalness as increased heterogeneity of participants, then the differing normative patterns of beliefs and overt behaviors lead to differing assumptions, different perceptions and different meanings for the stimuli (messages) in the situation. When the similarity of meanings is not achieved, then communication effectiveness is low. In a later chapter, some suggestions will be offered on how to reduce the probability of communication failure in this setting.

Principle #17—(a) The higher on the obligatory scale (must do or must not do) the topic of communication falls, the greater the probability of communication breakdown when the participants differ in their beliefs and behaviors related to that topic.

(b) The wider the range of allowed behaviors for all of the participants, the greater the range of topics on which they communicate effectively.

Taboos, as one form of strong obligatory injunction, were noted in Chapter 2. In the intracultural setting one is expected to know and adhere to the taboos. The sanctions against any violation of the taboos are very strong. Recently, the head of a Department of the U.S. Federal Government was forced to resign as a result of a communicative taboo involving sexual and bathroom preferences of an ethnic minority. In this case, the person probably knew that one in his position "ought not" to make that type of disparaging comment. He apparently was not aware of the potential hazard in exploiting the "must not" category; was careless in using it; and the sanctions against such a taboo forced his resignation.

While there might be some allowance for a violation of behaviors of the obligatory level in an intercultural situation, the offensiveness of a violation for the person whose norms had been violated would interfere with the continued transactions. Obviously, in the situation where knowledge of the "must do—must not do" behaviors is low or lacking, the risk of violating one of the norms is high.

Knowledge of and respect for the beliefs and overt behaviors of the other always is important for continued effective communication. Where the range of obligatory behaviors is wide and the range of allowed behaviors is relatively narrow, the risk of violation is very high with the very high probability of an ensuing communication breakdown. Thus, an important first step in preparing for communication in an intercultural situation is to become aware of the obligatory behaviors. Those behaviors which are considered appropriate but not necessarily obligatory are important to establish the best possible transaction; but a violation of these is more likely to be tolerated and less likely to cause a serious break in the communication.

It is conceivable that a violation of the "must do—must not do" behaviors of the other will result in an irreparable break in the transaction. This may happen with any number of persons from dyads to nations involved in the communication. Cultures also have rules for what one must do to re-establish a relationship that has been broken through violation of "must or ought" behaviors. By learning and following those rules, one may be able to mend broken transactions.

Principle #18—As level of knowing and accepting of the normative beliefs and overt behaviors by participants in a transaction moves from both knowing and both accepting to neither knowing and neither accepting, the difficulty of carrying on the transaction increases and the probability of communication breakdown increases.

The range of conditions in principle #18 is from most homogeneous to most heterogeneous. In Table 2, the thickness of the combined lines between the combinations of knowing and accepting for the two participants indicated the magnitude of the probable difficulty of communicating.

The claim here is that it is less critical not to know than to know and not accept. When either or both participants are not aware of the normative beliefs and overt behaviors of the other, they can, through their own transactions or in consultation with others, overcome the lack of knowledge quite readily. Established beliefs about what one must or must not do are more resistant to change, requiring much more time and intensive communication; and sometimes they are completely impervious to change.

Furthermore, it was claimed earlier that our beliefs determine the assumptions with which we approach a situation. If the transaction is between two persons (or groups) with similar beliefs, then their assumptions are expected to be similar. Thus, even if each does not know the beliefs of the other, they are more likely to be operating from a set of compatible assumptions than would be the case if they both know the beliefs of the other but did not accept those beliefs.

If the participants are tolerant of different beliefs on the part of the other, then the differences should not be insurmountable. Note, however, that the *value for tolerance* which is shared by the participants is a very significant point of similarity. Combine that with a shared belief that persons from different cultures should strive very hard for effective transactions and one has the two very critical shared beliefs in contributing to the probable success of communication efforts between them. That is a degree of homogeneity which can facilitate communication.

Each of the principles presented in this chapter can be illustrated more fully and will be in the remaining chapters. Hopefully, all of us will feel an obligation to test the validity of the model and principles which have been stated here.

One aspect of the model and of the principles stated here which is most urgently in need of test is whether the order of situations presented is an accurate description of ascending levels of heterogeneity. Which, if any, of the variables has the greatest impact on efficiency of communication as it changes toward more heterogeneity? Certainly the basic assumption that

heterogeneity of participants is negatively related to efficiency of communication also should be empirically validated.

These questions will guide me, and I hope others, to develop further
refinements of the notions presented in this and the preceding chapters.

EXERCISES

1. List at least three principles which you believe should be added to those in
   this chapter.
2. List three questions which you believe are most in need of research to add to
   our understanding of intercultural communication.
3. What would you hypothesize as the most likely findings of studies designed
   to answer those questions?
4. How would those findings change the way people generally approach communicating with highly heterogeneous others?
5. How would the findings change the way people generally approach communicating with homogeneous others?
6. How would you respond to a claim that there is a theory of intercultural
   communication as distinct from a general theory of communication?
7. Show slides of several metropolitan centers of the world. See if people can
   identify the country in which each of the cities is located. What similarities
   and what differences did you and others find among the various cities?
8. Show slides of people in several different styles of dress. What inferences do
   you draw about the people from their dress?

5

The Family and the Rabbits—

An Intracultural Transaction

The Level 1 communication is the most highly intracultural among all levels developed in Chapter 3. It represents the highest level of homogeneity which we can imagine. The hypothetical event selected to illustrate that level is a conversation between a happily married couple in a middle class American home. They are discussing the request of a daughter to buy a pair of rabbits and raise rabbits. The setting is a dyad using direct channels to consider a decision that will affect both of them and the others in the family.

THE PARTICIPANTS

The taxonomic description of the two participants, taken from Table 4, is as follows:

$$PRI_1 - CS_1 - KA_1 - WV_1$$

To elaborate that taxonomic description, I will take each set of the variables in sequence and report several of the elements of similarity which make these participants a Level 1 case.

First, the perceived relationship and intent for the transaction is highly positive and virtually identical. This perception tends to be a continuing one for these persons and not unique to this particular transaction. Even at times of frustration and annoyance with the other, the generally positive tone of the relationship predominates. Since the items are usually identical for both husband and wife, most items will be listed only once and not put into two separate columns, as will be done with more heterogeneous participants in later chapters.

Husband / Wife

PRI₁ (Perceived relationship and intent):
- Each perceives the other as thoughtful, considerate, kind, and loving.
- Both believe they plan together and do things well together.
- Both believe it's easy to talk person-to-person with the other.
- Both believe the other is willing to share and help as needed in various activities in which they and others in the family engage.

77

- Each believes the other senses how he/she feels most of the time.
- Both believe they encourage each other to learn and to grow.
- Both believe that when the other has a different idea as to what is best, the other does not try to force it on the partner, but is willing to consider other alternatives.

CS₁ (Code system):
- Both know and use standard U.S. Midwest English. The wife also speaks some Spanish, and the husband knows a few words of Spanish.
- Both know a few words and phrases in Japanese and Italian.

KA₁ (Knowledge and acceptance of normative beliefs and overt behaviors):
- Always be loyal and loving within the family.
- Disagreements should be settled fairly and rationally.
- Others' needs/wishes are to be respected, even if not accommodated.
- Parents should be models for children and others in the community.
- Be democratic, not autocratic.
- Each person should get a job and pay his own way.
- Keep informed on current public affairs and participate in the political process.
- Persons in the family should receive as good or better treatment than anyone else from each of us.
- Dress neatly; speak kindly; spend time doing things together.

The predominant structural level of values for both persons is stage five at Kohlberg's level three. At this level and stage, right action tends to be defined in terms of general individual rights and standards which have been critically examined and agreed upon by the whole society. There is emphasis on a legal point of view, but with the possibility of changing the law under rational consideration of social utility.

The values content for both persons includes: Family security; freedom with responsibility; equality; love; wisdom; intelligence; self-discipline; self-reliance; honesty; frugality; ecological balance and conservation of resources; cooperation; continuing growth in the mental, physical, social, and spiritual domains; and world peace.

Roles

Husband	*Wife*
Loving husband and father	Loving wife and mother
University professor	Elementary school teacher
Political campaign worker	Worker in League of Women Voters
Gardener	Good cook and food preserver
Flower grower	Flower arranger

Several roles are common to both. These include: student; friendly, helpful neighbor; informed citizen; church member; and bridge player.

WV$_1$ (World view):

- Both believe that life is a process of continuing growth, maturation, regeneration, etc.
- That most people can be trusted; we all earn trust by the way we behave; and that death is a natural part of the life processes.
- Both believe that the purpose of life is to: learn more about the universe and the balance required for life to continue; work with nature to leave the earth a better place in which to live; reduce hunger, disease, ignorance, hostility, selfishness, and greed.
- Both believe that *Homo sapiens* is a unique creature in the universe in that he can exert some control over the processes of life; he exists as part of a master plan; and that there is some universal force which may be referred to as the ultimate source of all being.

Hopefully, the data presented regarding the two participants is sufficient to establish the homogeneity of characteristics they share, and confirm that this is a Level 1 situation. With these characteristics identified, it is time to look at the transaction. It may be that those of you who have been in the situation of deciding whether or not to buy animals for a member of the family will find some similarities between your own situation and that reported here.

THE TRANSACTION

Prior to the transaction used here, the daughter had pleaded with both parents to buy a pair of rabbits and raise rabbits for sale. Both parents had resisted, saying that they weren't sure the daughter was ready to assume the responsibility of caring for them. Neither had unequivocally said it was impossible, leaving a glimmer of hope in the daughter's mind. One night after dinner, the husband and wife were still sitting at the dinner table, when the husband looked up after a rather lengthy and reflective silence.

"Betty, I feel we need to talk about Lisa's wanting those rabbits. I've been thinking about it quite a lot, and I have sensed that you have been too, even though you objected strongly to the idea when she first mentioned it."

"Yes, Ed, I have. I agree that in all fairness to Lisa, we must give her an answer. You're right. I did object and I still have some doubts."

"It would cost about $25.00 for a buck and a doe; feed would not be very expensive; we could build some hutches from the scrap lumber; there might be some veterinary bills, but I don't think of other costs now. She could probably handle the costs from her babysitting money."

"She could do that, if she will put her mind to it. One of my big concerns is that she'll lose interest after awhile, then we'll be expected to care for the rabbits. I'm afraid she won't get them fed and the pens cleaned regularly."

"I thought that might be part of the reason for your objections. We could sell them if that happens."

"We say that, but she'll complain, and promise to do better and it will just be another source of contention."

"I feel like we ought to take that chance. I think the rabbits would be good for her. It would give her something constructive to do rather than always wanting to go to the shopping center with that gang of kids. Also there's something about taking care of animals that can help develop a sense of responsibility. I think she is gentle with animals and would learn to care for them quickly. She also would need to learn about handling the baby rabbits and work out plans for marketing them. I think she could and would do that. It would give her a good sense of achievement."

"She certainly needs that. I'd like to think this might do it, but she doesn't seem to hold interest long enough in anything to see any positive result. I'm afraid the same might happen here. Do you think that if she pays for them and the other expenses she might feel more committed and retain her interest? If she could make some profit that would help too."

"I think that could help. It would be her project more than anything she's done before. It will give her someplace besides the pin ball machines to spend her babysitting money. She also said she would like to use the money she had in the bank to pay for them. That would help her feel more responsibility for them."

"How's she going to learn how to care for them?"

"They have a class at school in which they learn how to care for small animals. I think they teach students how to care for rabbits in that course. That could make school more interesting for her too."

"I can see you would like for her to have the rabbits and I would too. I think there's still the risk that she'll lose interest, but it could be worth taking the chance if it helps her find something to work for and feel good about. I think it probably will do that. Why don't we sit down with her and talk over how we can arrange to buy them and what it will cost her and what she has to be willing to do. I don't want them to become yours to feed and care for and hers to sell. We need to have some things understood about what she's to do, what we'll help her do, and what she can expect to get out of a rabbit project."

"I like that idea. Let's do it tomorrow evening if we're all available. We'll need an understanding, too, about how many females she can keep and how to handle the sales for meat and breeding stock. You'll have the major part of the driving to the market and to the feed store for feed and other supplies."

"I'll be willing to do that. I'll tell her after school tomorrow that we'll sit down after dinner and talk with her about buying the rabbits. I hope it works out all right."

"I think it will. We'll have to work out a good plan tomorrow night. That will be an important first step."

The outcome of the transaction by this time is no doubt apparent. Lisa does get the rabbits, uses her money from the bank to buy them; and agrees to help build the hutches, and take the class at school to learn how to raise rabbits. She is excited almost beyond description, and she does develop strong attachments for the animals, keeps the pens cleaned and the rabbits fed. She plays with them often, and she starts reading and writing about rabbits in her classes at school. There are some lapses in interest, but some reminders of their dependence on her for their care seemed to be enough to maintain her care of them. Money from sales helped maintain interest too.

ANALYZING THE TRANSACTION

Predictably, the husband and wife in the dialogue indicated similar feeling and desires about the rabbit buying decision. There were instances where each expressed what he/she thought the other felt and it was confirmed by the other. That level of sharing of feeling and confirmation would be expected and is the kind of transaction that helps achieve effective communication and builds homogeneity. That is not to say there were no differences in points of view.

Note that they used direct expressions of feeling, such as "I feel ..." It was a comfortable owning of feelings and beliefs that was expressed in the dialogue. The husband opened the transaction by stating his need to talk with the wife about the decision. Each brought data and opinions to the transaction which the other was willing to consider.

It is predictable, too, that each could often anticipate the response of the other to a comment. There are indications of a high level of empathy between the two; e.g., each had anticipated that the other was wanting to talk about the decision. We would expect that a number of nonverbal cues would have helped in that assessment.

An analysis of the content of the transaction would reveal several of the normative beliefs and behaviors had been included. Among these are the closeness of family ties and concern for fairness; self-reliance and responsibility; being able to pay one's own way; growth; personal worth; being democratic through including Lisa in aspects of the decision and through the sharing of the decision between husband and wife without either dominating the process.

With the level of homogeneity represented in this situation, the code system, both verbal and nonverbal, would be highly similar and the meanings elicited would be as nearly the same as is humanly possible. There was no strong need for feedback here beyond that provided when each would build the next statement off the prior statement of the other.

Reflected in the dialogue is a nurturing parent wishing to help the daughter have a good experience and good life. There is data gathering on how to bring this about, and consideration of consequences of the decision. And there is the excitement of happiness which a child would feel from having her own rabbits and learning to care for them. Along with this, too, there was concern for others in the family. The balance between sharing feelings, data gathering, and assessing outcomes is important in achieving effective communication.

What has been noted here in discussing the transaction is part of good communication in any situation. However, it occurs most easily among highly homogeneous participants. It may, in fact, be so automatic that there is little awareness of all that does occur.

When a communication breakdown occurs, the ability to talk about the communication that has occurred offers the best hope of fixing the breakdown and returning to the establishment of satisfying interdependent activity. This communicating about our communication is what is called metacommunication. It too is easier to do in the homogeneous situation.

In the metacommunication, it is important to clarify the intent of each and how each feels in the situation. Both should check their own assumptions and the assumptions of the other. This may involve looking at the beliefs and behaviors they believed were appropriate for the situation. It would ask what data were used and what assumptions are being made about the quality of the data. If there are different assumptions operating, what is the base for the difference and how can it be resolved?

Sometimes in a breakdown, an argument will develop about what a word or a symbol means. A better way of approaching this is to ask the other person what the word or nonverbal symbol means to him/her. This is a query that is more likely to occur where there is language heterogeneity, in that different meanings are expected in that case. The assumption often is made between homogeneous participants that they share more common meanings in the given context than is actually the case.

An opening to metacommunication may simply be: I have a feeling that we aren't communicating; or I feel we're not understanding one another. Do you feel that too? What is it that's happening?

The points mentioned above and others will be considered further as we move into more heterogeneous situations.

EXERCISES

1. Describe a transaction between two of the most homogeneous persons you know.
   a. What differences did you notice between this transaction and one involving two more heterogeneous persons whom you've observed?
   b. How were disagreements resolved in each instance, and how long did it take?
2. Can persons or groups, who are highly homogeneous at one point in time, experience a loss in homogeneity?
   a. If so, how does this occur?
   b. How do two or more persons achieve high level of homogeneity?
   c. What must persons and groups do to maintain a high level of homogeneity once it is attained?
3. What proportion of your transactions do you believe operate at this highest level of homogeneity?
4. How many families do you believe reach this level?

6

Separate Environments, Reduced Homogeneity, and Ease of Transactions

The illustration selected for a transaction at Level 2 of homogeneity-heterogeneity is of a couple who had been highly homogeneous before attending separate colleges.

Jim and Mary had lived in the same neighborhood for several years, had gone to school together and when they were both 17 years old they started dating. Their courtship had been a very pleasant one. They had shared many experiences together and their beliefs and patterns of behavior were very similar. When it was time to go to college, Jim went to a small conservative school which supported many of the norms they both had held quite firmly. Mary, through the encouragement of one of her teachers, selected a small liberally oriented college which had a program of social service work combined with courses on the campus. It provided experiences which were very new and different for Mary.

Before leaving for their respective colleges, Mary and Jim would have been at Level 1 of homogeneity. After two years, they still share a common world view in most respects, but their values and other normative beliefs have moved apart. Their relationship and intent toward one another is generally positive and they continue to share a common code system. The transaction reported here occurred one weekend when they were both home from college; and it deals with some proposed social action programs on women's rights and human sexuality.

THE PARTICIPANTS

The taxonomic description of their present level of homogeneity-heterogeneity is:

$$PRI_1 - CS_1 - KA_2 - WV_1$$

PRI₁ (Perceived relationship and intent):

Both participants perceive the other as having basically positive feelings toward self and the other. There is some annoyance when they become involved in discussions of topics on which they do not agree, but not at all negative.

At one level they both have goals of improving the living conditions of people in their community. They have different notions as to how to achieve that goal and sometimes overlook the goals they both share.

Each sees the other in an equal status and relationship; each respects the judgment and knowledge of the other. They have always been careful to avoid any sense of superior-subordinate in their relationship to one another.

Their experiences have confirmed that each has intentions of sharing with and helping each other. This is not to say that there have never been uncomfortable situations developing between them, but there have not been deliberate attempts to make the other feel uncomfortable or to injure the other.

CS₁ (Code system):

Both participants speak and write fluent standard American English. Neither has studied a foreign language and neither has developed facility in any of the dialects within the society.

KA₂ (Knowledge and acceptance of normative beliefs and overt behaviors):

Both participants know the beliefs and behaviors of the other, but they have reached a point where each feels that there are many beliefs of the other which they no longer can adhere to.

Before going to college, both believed quite strongly that the basic role of the woman in society was that of mother and homemaker. Jim still believes that just as strongly; Mary, on the other hand, now believes women should have the right to choose whether they want to be mothers. She believes that it is perfectly acceptable for a women to decide that she would rather work outside the home and hire someone to take care of the house and the children, if they have children.

Jim believes that parents are the only ones who should teach children about sex and that schools and churches should not intrude on that right. Mary, on the other hand, now believes that sex education classes must be offered in the schools, including discussion of contraceptives. For Jim, this is a taboo topic except between spouses; and between mother and daughter, and father and son at a time when they are approaching marriage.

Both believe that one should respect one's parents and other persons. This respect is shown through politeness and helpfulness. A person ought to help those in need and always behave toward another in the way that "I would want to be treated."

Both have been at Kohlberg's Level 2 of value structure, believing that rules are important for the well being of everyone in society; and people ought to follow the rules, not for fear of punishment, but because it's the thing to do for the good of society. Mary has been moving out a bit further in her consideration of values, giving more thought to universal principles of justice and fairness toward which all persons could strive.

The values content for both includes: education, freedom, equality, wisdom, self-discipline, self-reliance, honesty, world peace, improved standards of living for all the world, and tolerance for differing points of view. Mary holds somewhat more strongly to the value of tolerance than does Jim.

WV₁ (World view):

Both believe that life is fantastically complex—physically, socially, and psychologically. All of life is synchronized in amazing ways which are beyond the realm of the finite mind. Even so, humans learn more and more about it and gain increasing control over some parts of it. With the infinite possibilities, we probably will never know more than a small fraction of the total set of relationships we call life.

The purpose of life is to improve the human condition for all persons. We should, above all, strive to reduce hunger, poverty, and disease—both physical and mental. One way of achieving those purposes is to learn more and more about the universe and achieve more control. What one generation learns can contribute to what the next generation can achieve; that is what provides continuity to life.

They believe that in relation to the cosmos, any single individual is infinitesmally small. Yet each does exercise some influence. The human powers of reason can provide a significant force in working with nature to provide a continuing renewal and recycling process within the universe.

THE TRANSACTION

This transaction occurs one weekend when Mary and Jim are both home with their parents. Jim has gone to Mary's house for dinner and they're planning to get together with some of their friends after dinner. At dinner they have reminisced about their high school friends and experiences they had with them. Now the conversation has turned to what they have found most interesting at college. Mary is telling about some programs which she and other girls in her dorm have been involved in. One of these is a group considering sex education programs for high school students. Another is working to continue moves for more equality for women in the society.

MARY: This group on women's rights got a lot of us discussing what we want to do with our lives.

JIM: And what did you decide?

MARY: We want to feel free to choose whether or not to become mothers and homemakers or have a career in business, industry, or government.

JIM: You mean you'd consider not getting married and not having a family?

MARY: And why not? Some women have done this, but men keep trying to discourage them.

JIM: But how do you expect to have a fulfilled life if you don't marry and have children? That's woman's primary role!

MARY: Why do you say that's woman's *primary* role? That's only one of the roles she's capable of performing well. Are you saying that women can't handle the decisions of the business and governmental world as well as men?

JIM: I didn't say that.

MARY: Just what did you mean?

JIM: I mean that it's important for women to have children and care for them as every good mother should. If that doesn't happen, if lots of women start feeling that way, the whole human race could become extinct.

MARY: I don't think there's much chance of that. Besides, I'm not saying that women shouldn't marry and have children. I'm saying that there are other things they can do which are equally or more important.

JIM: What could be more important than being a good wife and mother?

MARY: What do you think is involved in being a good wife and mother? Is it staying home and cleaning the house, doing laundry, cooking, and playing with the kids? Or is there something more?

JIM: Is there anything wrong with that? Those are pretty important for a family. And playing with the kids, that's really important in their development.

MARY: And I suppose I'm to be mainly responsible for that development. What about the father's responsibility in the development of the kids?

JIM: I'm not sure what's happening to you at that school, but I'm getting bothered by whatever it is.

MARY: I notice that you didn't answer the question about the father's responsibility. You just said you don't like my starting to think about and question the way people in this neighborhood think about "woman's place."

Jim and Mary continue the discussion and find themselves discussing aspects of life they had never really talked about in this way before. Jim becomes more and more annoyed with Mary's ideas. Mary also talks about her visits to some schools where "innovative" sex education programs are in operation. Jim becomes quite uncomfortable talking about this topic and he feels very strongly that this is not an appropriate role for the schools. With the strong beliefs he has held on this topic, he merely says it definitely is not something the schools should be doing; that it just gets kids all aroused and experimenting with sex before they are married and that just leads to all kinds of problems.

Mary tells Jim this is a very narrow view; that kids have always experimented with sex and the opportunities to do so are much greater now than they were 50 or so years ago ... that it's being very naive to think about the way he is. She argues that the only way to deal with promiscuity, unwanted children, and all the problems associated with unwanted children is extensive sex education programs in every school. Mary asserts that she is going to work with groups of students and adults who believe as she does to try to get sex education programs established in more of the school systems in the state.

Jim shakes his head in annoyance and frustration. He has difficulty believing this is the same person he took to the senior prom less than a year ago. Inwardly he is deciding to work against the ideas Mary is supporting. He and Mary both are feeling some strain in the transaction; each would like to influence the other's beliefs on these topics, but it's time to go meet their friends. So the discussion of these topics must be suspended, at least for the present.

They enjoy the visit with their friends where more of the conversation deals with past experiences and social issues. Mary finds the evening somewhat less exciting than she had hoped. ... Future transactions between Mary and Jim on the topics of women's roles and sex education tend to further intensify the positions expressed in the aforementioned segment of the transaction. And the eager anticipation of seeing one another on weekend visits to their parents gradually declines.

ANALYZING THE TRANSACTION

The participants have shared many experiences in the past with relatively high agreement and shared goals. They approach the transaction here with the perception of continuing high compatibility. There may have been a latent desire on Mary's part to change the commonly accepted definition of the role of women. However, there had been no prior discussions among her close friends or her parents and their friends challenging the role definition expressed by Jim.

They have essentially the same values. While they have not discussed values openly, the behaviors practiced have given confirmation of the values for each of them. As they have pursued the separate programs at the separate colleges, the definition of "good" education has shifted for Mary as she has been exposed to several courses in human behavior, especially those dealing with individual and societal relationship. Jim, in his physical science program, has been more heavily involved in courses in mathematics, chemistry, and physics. Thus, he has not been involved to an appreciable extent in discussions of some of the more controversial issues such as the role of women and sex education.

Jim seems quite surprised, perhaps even startled, by Mary's positions on the role of women and sex education. He has difficulty understanding how she could accept the beliefs she expressed in the transaction. He seems unwilling to consider alternatives which deviate from what he has learned and hoped that Mary shared. Mary, who believes that Jim generally is tolerant of others' beliefs, is puzzled by his one-sided position on the role of women. The intensity of their involvement with the topic is possibly related to the bearing that this issue has on their own continuing relationship. The fact that they are relatively homogeneous on most dimensions permits them to shift to other activities and have an enjoyable evening.

At this level of homogeneity-heterogeneity, one of the basic questions is whether participants can tolerate, even if they don't fully accept, the beliefs and behaviors of another which conflict with their own normative beliefs and behaviors. Mary's statements might have been less threatening to Jim if their relationship had been one of casual friendship rather than one of courtship. This may illustrate how the perceived intensity of the relationship in addition to the positiveness or negativeness also will influence the nature of the communication and its outcomes. There appear to be shared goals in areas other than the role of women and who should provide programs of sex education. It also appears that they can operate as equals in a transaction on a topic on which they have differing beliefs.

The code system seems to present no special difficulty. There is some uncertainty of meaning in most transactions. At one point Mary asks for clarification. This seeking of feedback to improve consensuality of meaning is important in all transactions. The effort required to achieve that consensus increases as the heterogeneity of the participants increases.

It is apparent that the difference in norms regarding the role of women and what constitutes appropriate sex education has resulted in a somewhat less satisfying transaction than would have resulted had they held the same beliefs and subscribed to the same behaviors regarding these two topics. Mary seems to want to help Jim to understand and accept her position on the two topics; and Jim seems to want to help Mary to understand and accept his position. Each presumably would like the other to support and work for a common goal; hence some persuasion is undertaken to bring the other to one's own position.

Both share the concern for the well-being of others, for honesty, freedom, education, wisdom, and improved standards of living. These values provide the common base from which they can discuss the "must, ought, allowed, ought not, and must not do" in relation to the issues discussed in the transactions. If we were to ask Mary and Jim to state the norms about how a son or daughter or father or mother should behave, we undoubtedly would get agreement regarding many of the behaviors, indicating reasonably high homogeneity. As stated earlier, they each generally know the normative beliefs and behaviors of the other; and they accept many of them. But, in the aspects of life included in the transaction, neither person at this time is ready to accept and adhere to the behaviors proposed by the other.

To further clarify Jim's beliefs, Mary could have asked whether he was expressing a desired pattern of behavior for all women or whether he was stating the role he would want for his own wife. She could probe for the boundaries. Jim, on the other hand, could ask Mary whether she was describing what she wants for her own life; or whether she is saying that all women should be more free of social, economic, and other pressures in deciding how to define their own roles. Each also could have clarified the boundaries for what they called sex education, what they wanted it to achieve, and how that might influence decisions as to who can best conduct it.

Their common world view is not incompatible with the positions either is taking on the two issues. For their continued satisfaction in future transactions, it could be very helpful for them to focus on some of their similarities of beliefs and goals along with those on which they differ. They also will need to explore how much tolerance they have for what kind of differences. Their answer to that question and to what differences and similarities they see between themselves will help them predict the outcomes and efficiency of their future transactions.

EXERCISES

1. What changes, if any, have you made within the past year in your beliefs about what a person who is an accepted member of your culture:
   a. Must do?
   b. Ought to do?
   c. Is allowed to do?
   d. Ought not do?
   e. Must not do?
2. What changes, if any, have you made within the past year in your beliefs about:
   a. The nature of life?
   b. The purpose of life?
   c. The relation of man to the cosmos?
3. How have those changes in items one and two, if any, affected your communication:
   a. With persons in your own culture?
   b. With persons from other cultures?
4. What kind of communication experiences do you believe may produce changes in normative beliefs and behaviors, and in world view?
5. If you were involved in a situation such as that described in Chapter 6, what would you do to facilitate future communication:
   a. If you were Mary?
   b. If you were Jim?
   c. If you were a friend of Mary or Jim?

7

The Teacher and the Drop-outs—

An Intermediate Case

This communication event is at the midpoint (Level 4) of the seven levels of heterogeneity. At this level, using the taxonomic scheme, one of the variables is at the heterogeneous end of the continuum, one is at the homogeneous end, and two are near the middle of the continuum. The specific category selected has the perceived relationship and intent toward the homogeneous end, the world view toward the heterogeneous end, and the other two near the mid-point. Another possibility, not as yet developed in the taxonomic scheme presented in Table 4, would be to have all variables near the midpoint on the homogeneity-heterogeneity continuum.

The example chosen to illustrate this level is that of a white, middle class school teacher about 60 years old talking with a group of five inner city youths at a "drop-in center" in a lower income area of a USA city. The teacher would like to persuade the youths to come back to school and use their talents in "constructive" ways, and not waste themselves on the "disruptive" ways they're now following.

It is another direct channel situation with one person of one cultural milieu and five persons of another cultural milieu.

THE PARTICIPANTS

The taxonomic description of the participants is:
$$PRI_1 - CS_2 - KA_2 - WV_2$$
The participants have had some prior contact in the high school in which the teacher teaches. The result of that contact has been to establish a positive perceived relationship between them. They have learned enough about each other to have a fairly good idea of the normative beliefs and overt behaviors of each. They don't accept the normative patterns of beliefs and overt behaviors of the other; but they have a value which allows them to tolerate the difference and still communicate.

They also have found that quite different views of the nature and purpose of life exist between teacher and youth. Their views of the cosmos and the relation of humans to it also differ appreciably.

91

The youths refer to the teacher somewhat fondly as "teach." This is a salutation they learned from peers before they'd had any face-to-face contact with the teacher themselves.

PRI₁ (Perceived relationship and intent):

Teacher	*Youth*
These are really good people. I'd like to help them develop their talents so that they may have a better life than they've had thus far. I think they respect me and are willing to share some of their hopes and thoughts with me, things they don't talk to many others about. I feel I can talk to them on a serious person-to-person basis.	"Teach" will listen to us and not start scolding right away when we say or do something. "Teach" takes time to talk with us, even a little extra when we need it; doesn't treat us like little kids ... wants to help kids like us.

CS₂ (Code system):

The teacher and the youths all speak American English. The teacher has a more extensive vocabulary in standard English; the youths have a more extensive vocabulary of slang or idiomatic expressions. The youths have a well developed inner city dialect. The teacher has learned some of the dialect through contacts with students in school, but it's about the level of the American who learns a hundred words to use when visiting a foreign country.

KA₂ (Knowledge and acceptance of normative beliefs and overt behaviors):

Always be honest; say, "I can't talk about that," rather than falsify.	Be honest but don't tell everything if it gets you in trouble; it's O.K. to fake it a little.
Abstain from premarital sex.	Premarital sex is O.K. if you love the person.
Don't steal.	It's all right to take little things you need, but not from a friend.
Don't use profanity.	It's O.K. to swear. It sounds grownup and it's the best way to let people know how you feel.
Be an individual; don't be led around like sheep following the crowd.	Talk like the crowd, dress like the crowd, do what the crowd does or you'll be a nobody.
Don't drink alcoholic beverages, or use drugs.	Drink "booze" and smoke a little "pot" to show you're really with it and not a kid anymore.

Study hard and get a good job.

Work hard and succeed.

"Goof off" in school, even drop out; it doesn't help you later anyway. It's a bore.

Work as little as possible.

Values

Happiness	Pleasure
Freedom with responsibility	Freedom with low or no restraint
Tolerance	Tolerance with conditions
Peace and quiet	Noise and action
Maturity	Youth
Wisdom	Wealth
Intellectual achievement	Physical prowess
Pleasing personality	Physical attractiveness
Efficiency	"Style"

Roles

Teacher	Playful teenager
Informed citizen	Sportsfan
Tennis Club member	Pool player
Post-graduate student	School drop-out
Devoted spouse	Passionate lover
Planned Parenthood Assn. member	Clique member

WV₂ (World view):

Life can be thought of in both physical and social-psychological terms, even in metaphysical terms. Life is continuous, exciting, challenging, satisfying. We are affected by everything around us, and we have an effect on things around us.

The purpose of life is to develop one's potential to the fullest limit and help others to do the same; to explore and understand the universe and life of all kinds.

There's a high degree of interdependence between many, if not all, elements in the universe. *Homo sapiens* is the most highly developed creature in the universe, but doesn't always

Life is being born, getting hungry, cold, hot, tired, rested, pushed around, old, and dying. That's it. It's not much fun when you stop to think about it. It just is; you can't do much to change it.

The purpose of life is to get rich, have fun, and find ways of not having to work very much or very hard. Look out for oneself and let the other guy take care of himself.

There are more resources out there than we'll ever need; use all you want; get yours before somebody else does .... It's a waste of time to think about things like this; just take behave that way. *"Homo"* needs to work with nature to achieve a balance via recycling of energy and other resources. There's a continual process of change going on ever so slowly most of the time, with occasional dramatic spurts. *"Homo"* can affect that process somewhat, but much is beyond human control.

it as it comes and make the most of it.

THE TRANSACTION

Prior to the transaction reported here, the teacher and the youths had engaged in a limited discussion at school about the value of school. The youths had vehemently stated it was a waste of time and a bore. The teacher had little opportunity to respond and the youths had quit school. The teacher had sensed that these youths had a lot of energy and keen minds. "Teach," as the students called the teacher, decided to find out where the youths spent most of their time, then go there to talk with them.

The gathering point was a local "drop-in" recreation center where a number of school drop-outs and young unemployed people "hang out." It's rumored that there is regular drinking of beer and wine and perhaps some drug traffic. "Teach" had not been to this place before and feels a bit uneasy about going there. It's not a spot frequented by teachers from the local school.

In presenting the sample conversations, the youths will be identified as Y_1, Y_2, etc. The teacher will be identified by the name the youth have given, namely, "teach." As in the prior examples, the conversations will be abbreviated here. "Teach" enters the center and takes a few moments to adjust to the change in lighting, then looks around for the five youths. Finally, he spots a social case worker he has met at the school. He goes to the case worker and inquires about the youths. The case worker has seen two of them and offers to take "teach" over to a table where Y_1 and Y_2 are watching a card game. They move through a maze of bodies, male and female, draped over and around the tables and chairs in the place. As they come close to the table, Y_1 and Y_2 look up in surprise as "teach" greets them:

TEACH: Hi there.

Y_1 AND Y_2: Teach! 'Whatcha' doin' here?

CASE WORKER: He'd like to talk to you for awhile.

Y_1: With us? What about? School?

TEACH: Well, yes and some other things. Could we get a table and have some coffee or cokes?

Y_2: Who's buyin'?

TEACH: It's on me this time.

Y_1:   I guess it's worth a chance.

(At this point Y_3 and Y_4 and Y_5 come by and say almost together):

Hi teach.

TEACH: Hi gang. How're you getting along?

YOUTH TOGETHER: Cool man ... Cool.

TEACH: Will you join us for a coke? I'm buying.

(all sit at the table)

Y_3:   Hey teach, ain't you afraid comin' down here?

TEACH: Yes ... I must confess, I'm a little uneasy ... kind of nervous.

Y_4:   Why you here? Is it about us?

TEACH: Yes, it's about you, all of you. I was sad when you all dropped out of school.

Y_5:   You sad about us droppin' out? Ya hear that? Sad about us droppin' out.

Y_1:   I bet not many were sad; most of 'em probably happy to see us go.

TEACH: I suppose that's right. You five weren't always the quietest crew around. But for the last week or two, I've had this urge to talk to all of you. I tried calling your home but I couldn't find you there. I never could find a way of contacting you 'til one of the guys at school said I might find you here.

Y_2:   Why do ya' wanta talk to us? Not many people back there ever did.

Y_4:   Yea. Who sent you?

Y_5:   What's your angle? You wanta get us back in that cage? No way!

Y_1:   Aw come on. Give him a chance. He never was like the rest of them high an' mighties back there throwin' their weight around.

TEACH: I always thought you had what it takes to do something good if you just had the chance, and if you were willing to try.

Y_1:   We like what we're doin' now ... no books; no class schedules to keep; no hasslin' about what we do or don't do. We're doin' great ... just great.

Y_5:   Yea, and we have food and a place to sleep and some cats to party with, and a little hustlin' will get some spending money ... no time schedules. It's better than you have it "teach."

TEACH: Are you telling me you have everything right here that you'll ever want?

Y_4:   That's right! Everything!

Y_2:   It sure is better than bein' in that ole school.

Y_1:   Well ... it sure would be nice to have a fancy car so all the chicks would look up when I go by and wish that I'd ask 'em to go for a cruise ... and some fancy duds ... and a little extra "bread" so we could go to some of them fancy places with dinner and wine by candlelight.

Y_2:   Yea man. That'd be great. I'd love to show off to some of them back at school that always think they're so great.

TEACH: What would it take to have that happen?

Y_1:   I'd have to have a good job and a steady income, something my ole man never had. I just wish I could do it without having to punch the clock and do what somebody else tells me all the time.

Y_2:   Yea, me too. That's what's nice around here. Nobody tells ya' where ya' have to be when, or what you have to do when ya' get there. There's always some fun going on someplace.

TEACH: You wish there were jobs like that and maybe places to learn how to do that kind of work, legitimate work?

TWO OF THE Y'S IN CHORUS: Yea. I sure do. (The others were more hesitant.)

TEACH: What kind of things would you like to do? Y_1, you did some pretty good sketches when you were in class. Do you like to do that kind of thing?

Y_1:   Yea, that's fun; but what's that have to do with work?

TEACH: I thought you might like to do some commercial art. You might even have your own little shop so you could set your own hours. You could make signs for people. Do sketches for letters or books, or for posters. You might even want to think about working with some of the stores on window displays. What do you think about that kind of work?

Y_3:   The "teach" could get the big commission on all the jobs and you could do all the work ... huh teach? Not bad ...

TEACH: You all still don't quite trust me, I guess. You think I've got to have an angle. You don't believe anybody would do anything for you just because they wanted to help.

Y_3:   That's right. Everybody's got their angle.

TEACH: I promise you there's no angle. Will you at least give me a chance?

Y_3:   Well, maybe. It just seems funny that you'd do this without some hook in it someplace.

TEACH: How about it Y_1? Are you willing to take a look at some things you could do?

Y_1:   I don't know. I'm not sure I could do it. I just don't know enough about it.

TEACH: Would you like to find out more? I have a friend who does this. We could go visit his shop some time. I'd like to take you over there if you'd be willing.

Y_1:   I guess it wouldn't hurt ... I guess it'd be O.K. to check it out. It's gettin' kinda' crowded in here, let's go out and walk.

OTHER Y'S: Yea, lets. I'm beginning to feel like a fish in a fishbowl with them other cats starin' at us.

TEACH: I'm feeling like lots of people are staring at me too. Will they hassle you about talking with me? (as they walk out into the street)

Y_2:   Naw ... they'll wonder about what you wanted ... want to be sure you weren't gettin' on us about somethin'. Everybody here feels it's kinda up to you what ya do as long as ya don't get somebody else in a jam.

Y_3: Ya know teach, the thing I wish I could do sometime? (not waiting for an answer) I wish I could build things or fix 'em. I used to have fun fixin' chairs and tables that'd break. Everybody was surprised to find 'em in shape to use again. My ole man, when he was there, would try to fix em, but they'd break; same with my brothers. But me, a chick, I'd fix 'em and they'd stay. How about that?

TEACH: That's great. I know a little shop where I've had some chairs fixed and refinished. Would you like to stop by there some time?

Y_3: Yea. I think I might. That might be fun.

TEACH: I have an idea. Why don't I find a time when we would go to those two places. Maybe you'd all like to go see them, would you? I'll drive.

Y's: Yea. Sure.

TEACH: I feel excited about doing this with you. I hope you do too.

Y_1: I am ... I feel kinda funny too. How about the rest of ya?

Y's: (Respond with mixed reactions, but all agree that they'll go along and see what's there. It'll be something different to do anyway.)

TEACH: How do we get together again when I've got the time set up?

After some further talk as they walked to the corner, they agree on a time and place to meet again. Each agreed that after the initial nervousness they were glad that "Teach" had come down to the center. They're still suspicious. They have difficulty accepting that he'd care enough to do this without having some angle. People just don't act that way usually. Yet, he was kind of different than most of 'em back at school. He did seem to care.

ANALYZING THE TRANSACTION

The transaction is a moderately easy one for the participants, even with some barriers to overcome. The teacher is uneasy in a social setting to which he is not accustomed; the youth are uneasy with someone like the teacher in the setting in which they usually feel quite comfortable. However, the perceived relationship is positive enough to permit establishing reciprocally acknowledged attention and mutual responsiveness quite readily. The presence of the case worker as intermediary, no doubt, was helpful.

The mutual responsiveness becomes apparent when the teacher and the youth agree to find a table and have something to drink. It also occurs when the youth agree to talk with the teacher about whatever it is that he came to see them about. There is the period of testing trust to see whether it's all right to proceed.

There is evidence of congruent functional identity developing when the teacher anticipates the question of who's buying. It is further developed when the youths are willing to give "teach" the benefit of their doubt and go along with his interest in wanting to help them; and it continues to develop when "teach" anticipates that the youths probably could not or would not undertake and continue with any work or study which had rigid time demands initially. Finally they reach the stage where youth and teacher are imputing to self and other sequences of forthcoming activity—the plans to visit the shops and things they each must do to bring this about. At that point the functional identities have definitely become congruent and all can feel some satisfaction and success with the transaction.

The shared focus is finding out what's involved in improving their condition, exploring some alternatives which may help achieve some of their future goals, while still retaining some of what they like of what they already have.

To help with the transaction, the teacher wisely went through the case worker as a first step. The case worker, known to the youth and apparently trusted by them, could help alleviate some initial barriers. It might be necessary under more difficult conditions to draw more heavily on the case worker as an intermediary, both before and during the meeting of teacher and youths. The prior relationship, in this case, also had established a positive perception of the possible relationship and intent.

Each knew the norms, values, and roles of the others and recognized the difference between the teacher and the youths. Although not accepting the normative patterns of beliefs and overt behaviors of the other, there were some points of shared desires that could be identified under the general heading of a "better life" for the youths.

The teacher was direct and open in his statement of his feelings and intent, including his own nervousness. The youths also were direct in expressing their doubts and other feelings. There were shades of "bold front" in which they claimed everything was great, admitting they couldn't stand school, then admitting that they would like something better. At this point, the teacher, rather than giving a prescription, asked them what they would have to have change to get what they'd really like.

When the youths began to list some things they would like to do and would need to do to reach some different goals, the teacher could then begin posing some possibilities to explore. The teacher had done his homework well enough to have anticipated some things that some of the youths could do well and he assumed enjoyed doing. His assumption was supported; and as he recognized something the youths had done well, added a bit to their sense of achievement, especially Y_1, at first. Y_3 picked up on the conversation and shared in the sense of achievement by recalling how she was able to fix broken furniture. "Teach" alertly picked up on the feelings and with the youths developed some possibilities for combining what they liked with the goal of a job and some steady money.

An essential element for the transaction to occur was a willingness to accept and respect the differences they knew existed between them, even though neither could adhere to the norms and values of the other. Neither the youths nor the teacher criticized the other for their respective norms and values. There was an implicit recognition of the differences in what was talked about and what was not talked about. The things talked about were only those which had to be talked about by the teacher to achieve his goal and build the relationship necessary to even get that goal considered.

Note, too, as they begin to accept some possibility of exploring a new life style, a desire is expressed to get out of the center and walk. Part of this could be a physical moving out and away from real or imagined social pressure against the plans they're developing with "teach." They may be reducing one set of cultural barriers at the risk of increasing another set; at least that may be their perception at this time.

As the present base of trust is confirmed in future transactions, the relationship between "teach" and the youths would be expected to strengthen. As that happens, they may wish to and could talk explicitly about their differences in beliefs and the consequences of living out those beliefs ... consequences for themselves and others.

It should be obvious that the transaction would have been much more difficult to initiate and continue, if added to the specified differences between teacher and youths, the normative patterns of beliefs and overt behaviors were not known; or the languages were entirely different; or if the perceived relationship had been negative. The conclusion of the transaction would probably have been viewed as less satisfactory and less successful than it was.

EXERCISES

1. How would the transaction differ for taxonomic set No. 14 (PRI_2 CS_3 KA_1 WV_1) as compared to set No. 18 ($PRI_1 \bullet CS_2 \bullet KA_2 \bullet WV_2$) which was illustrated in this chapter?
2. How would the transaction differ for taxonomic set No. 23 (PRI_1 CS_1 KA_3 WV_2) as compared to set No. 18?
3. What difficulties would be most likely to occur and what would you do to cope with them?
4. How do you think the transaction would differ if all the variables were at some midpoint between the ends of the homogeneity-heterogeneity continuum for all the variables?
5. On which side of this midpoint would the majority of your transactions fall? To what extent would an intermediary be helpful in these transactions?

8

Wrong Ticket,
Different Language—
A Moderately
Heterogeneous Case

This Level 5 transaction is just past the midpoint toward the heterogeneous end of the continuum used in the taxonomy. The situation used here is an international one.

The communication event involves a husband and wife from the USA working out some travel arrangements with a travel agent from Xania. The hotel clerk where the Americans are staying in Xania has made reservations and provided prepaid tickets for a tour. Now there is some difficulty with the tickets and they are trying to resolve the difficulty with the Xanian travel agent.

THE PARTICIPANTS

The taxonomic description would show the heterogeneity on two variables and homogeneity on the other two sets. It is as follows:

$$PRI_1—CS_3—KA_3—WV_1$$

The participants, based on past experiences and present visible cues, have generally positive perceptions of one another and their intent toward one another. If they were able to check out world views, they would find high similarity; however, there are considerable differences in norms, values, and role expectations.

The differences noted above have some degree of national characteristics inherent; but all Americans and all Xanians should not be stereotyped according to the traits listed.

PRI₁ (Perceived relationship and intent):

Americans	*Xanian Travel Agent*
Most Xanians have been friendly and helpful. This man is smiling so he probably will be friendly and helpful too. The travel posters all say, "Welcome tourist," so they must want to cooperate with us.	Americans are usually friendly, sometimes boisterous and rude; but generally they are fair and cooperative. Besides these have been talking with the priest who was sitting behind them, so they must be good people. There are obnoxious ones, of course.

CS₃ (Code system):

The Americans have a pocket dictionary with translations between English and Xanian and vice versa. Their pronunciation of Xanian is clumsy and sometimes unintelligible to Xanians.

In his contacts with tourists the Xanian has learned a few words of English, but he does not have confidence in his use of English words or in their pronunciations. There sometimes is another agent on duty who is reasonably fluent in English, but he is gone.

KA₃ (Knowledge and acceptance of normative beliefs and overt behaviors):

Americans	*Xanians*
Be tolerant of others; especially make allowances for foreigners.	Strictly follow the rules and customs of the place where you are. ("When in Rome, do as the Romans do.")
Be trusting of others.	Be suspicious of anyone who is different.
Be honest and considerate.	Be honest and considerate.
Be adventuresome.	Be cautious.
Wear whatever is comfortable.	Wear whatever is customary, i.e., the style.
Say what you believe.	Say what's proper, be careful not to offend.
Work hard and don't waste time visiting on the job.	Be conscientious in your work, but have time for people, even if that means stopping to talk to them.
Level one value structure seems dominant for these people. They believe that an extra tip will get rules relaxed and this is all right. The	Level two value structure is dominant. He believes everyone should follow the rules explicitly and not give nor expect favors. Values con-

values content includes: honesty; independence; freedom; individuality; democratic decision making; industrial technology; physical strength and beauty.

tent includes: honesty; obedience; discipline; professional ethics; art; handcraftsmanship; music; authority; nature; family security; and autocratic decision making.

Roles

As seen by self—Important person; good parent; deeply religious; kind and thoughtful traveler; civic leader; business leader.
As seen by the other—another tourist; rich American; souvenir collector; big spender.

As seen by self—Conscientious worker and servant of people; good parent; upright citizen; good model for my country; kind but firm man.
As seen by other—Officious bureaucrat; average person.

WV₁ (World view):

Both the Americans and the Travel Agent believe in a monotheistic diety in the Judaic-Christian tradition, a diety that has formed and directs the universe. They believe that people are basically alike; however, in practice they may not always behave consistently with that belief. They believe the world is beautiful and good; and that God has given man power and wisdom to control the universe. They believe each individual is unique and important. They believe the purpose of life is to increase one's faith in the diety and to do good works to inherit eternal life. To have the best life, one delays gratification. They accept the view that man should exercise careful stewardship over the earth's resources; but again practice may not be entirely consistent with the belief.

THE TRANSACTION

A transaction approximating the following was overheard in a travel office in Xania. The American couple had been talking to a priest sitting beside them in the waiting room while awaiting their turn to talk to the travel agent. The priest had studied in America about three years prior to this event and had learned some English during that time, but had not used it recently and welcomed the opportunity to practice his English. His English was quite slow and haltingly spoken as he would search for words. The Americans were attempting a few phrases of Xanian in reply.

A representative of the hotel which the American couple were using as a base had worked out the itinerary for their trip and bought the tickets. He arranged with a friend in the town the couple were visiting (about 600 kilometers away) to complete the return reservations. When the couple arrived at the agency for the final confirmation of their return reservations, the class of travel had been changed, and there was a claim for an additional tax. They had been told by the friend of the hotel representative that all arrangements were in order as initially requested and everything was completely paid for.

The American man hands his tickets to the agent, the agent smiles, looks over the tickets, consults a chart and speaks to the Americans. The Americans hear "first class ... (some other words) and 250 zechls." (About $15 U.S.). The American in his meager Xanian vocabulary attempts to say "All paid; second class." He also takes out his pocket dictionary and begins to look through the set of frequently needed phrases. The travel agent speaks some sentences at regular speed in Xanian, something which the Americans cannot translate. They use the Xanian word for "do not comprehend."

The travel agent repeats some more words with a little higher volume and the Americans reddening from embarrassment and annoyance again shake their heads and say, "do not comprehend." They begin looking again at the dictionary, while shaking their heads and asking for someone who speaks English. At this point, the priest who is nearby comes to the rescue and speaks to the travel agent for a few moments. He then turns to the Americans and in his slow, halting English explains that the tickets say first class; that the travel agent does not wish to change the tickets because it would leave an unsold reservation in first class; and that no federal transport tax has been paid on the tickets.

The Americans explain to the priest that they do not have enough zechls to pay the difference in fare and the tax and that the arrangement was made and reconfirmed by the friend at the hotel just yesterday. They had been assured that everything was in order as requested and all paid. The priest then explains this to the travel agent. The travel agent replies that he only knows what his chart and the tickets show. Both show that it is first class, there is additional fare due, and the tax has to be paid.

It is getting closer and closer to train time. People in the line are impatiently shifting from one position to another and their voices sound agitated to the Americans. The agent is frowning and alternately tapping his hands and the tickets on the counter. The American man has taken enough zechls from his pocket to pay the tax. His is visibly holding it in his hand, but not moving it toward the agent.

The Americans ask the priest to ask the agent to please change the tickets to second class and to explain that they cannot understand what has happened, since they were assured twice prior to today that everything was in order and completely paid. After a somewhat lengthy conversation between the priest and the agent with very serious expressions on their faces, but seemingly patient with each other, the priest says that the agent can change the ticket to second class but that the tax will have to be paid. The priest's English is such that the American couple and he have to repeat sentences, and often must choose other words to express their thoughts in order to achieve understanding.

The travel agent has told the priest that the correction of any error regarding the tax will have to be made at the point of origin. The couple reluctantly pay the tax, graciously thank the priest, smile weakly to the travel agent, who also manages a slight smile as the couple receive their tickets and car assignment and move away from the window. The priest then directs them to the appropriate gate and the platform for their train. He also carefully writes some directions on a slip of paper and suggests that they hand this to the conductor. Since conductors all wear a standard uniform, they should now be able to get along.

As they approach the gate, they pause to look at their tickets, check the piece of paper given them by the priest, and look at the signs on the gates. At that point a Xanian coming by pauses and asks in fluent English if he can help them. Their behavior apparently signaled some confusion. They tell him their destination and he says he also is going there and if they wish to follow him he will help them get on the correct car. The train terminates at their destination so they do not have to worry about getting off at the appropriate stop.

For those of you who have had a similar experience, you can empathize with the warm feeling the couple must have had when they again could talk with the representative at their hotel. That's especially true when that representative has been most gracious and efficient in all other arrangements. These persons can point out things to avoid which are overly costly; places to see and places to avoid; and offer many helpful tips on how to see more things for less money. These persons also can be very helpful in handling the problems of limited language facility.

ANALYZING THE TRANSACTION

Perhaps the most obvious aspect of the transaction just described is the sense of sheer helplessness of participants in a situation where they do not have a common code nor any translator. The operation of principle #18[1] is well illustrated by this incident.

While the nonverbal code has been noted in each of the transactions, the reliance on it was probably greater in the Level 5 case described here. than in any of the others. Note the assumption of the universal expressions of emotion. This included the facial expressions indicating friendliness, frustration, annoyance, embarrassment and being very serious. The hand tapping and body movement were indicators of tension, impatience, and annoyance.

This very likely was one of the less happy moments for the American couple in their visit to Xania. The outcome seemed less than satisfying to them. Their world view and that of the travel agent would lead them to

[1]Principle #18—If the participants do not share a common code system (both verbal and nonverbal) or have a mechanism for translating into a common code, then the desired communication becomes impossible.

identify the priest as an intermediary whom both could trust. Undoubtedly the situation would have been much more traumatic without the aid of a considerate intermediary.

You will recall that in the Level 4 case it was suggested that the case worker's very brief role as intermediary probably was helpful in establishing a satisfying transaction. Both of these cases should begin to suggest the increasing value of an effective intermediary as the communication situation becomes more highly intercultural.

Without the aid of the intermediary, it is doubtful if the participants would have been able to establish mutual responsiveness. They, with the aid of the priest, were able to get the tax fee to the agent and the ticket cleared and travel space assigned for the couple to get back to the town in which they were living.

The sense of embarrassment and helplessness communicated by facial expressions and attempts to use the dictionary would be expected to communicate a sense of helplessness to the travel agent. No report of his feelings or his perception of the couple's feelings is available. We can only project from our own experiences. His norms still hold him to following the rules, as well as being suspicious of someone who is different and certainly Americans are different than Xanians. Yet, his norms which say, "Be considerate, say what's proper and be careful not to offend," require him to deal patiently and politely with the couple. Their norms for "being trusting and tolerant of others" would require that they not confront the agent in an obnoxious way.

The smiles may have been taken to mean let's be friends, I want to do what's right. They may be able to smile in a situation of this type as a result of believing that the world is essentially beautiful and good; and for the American couple that one should be able to delay gratification. The delayed gratification may occur if the hotel representative can untangle the tax fee more satisfactorily later.

The similar assumptions deriving from similar world views are helpful. The differing assumptions, which would derive from different norms, values, and role expectations, can be tempered by the intermediary who is somewhat bi-cultural.

Note the use of the written message given by the priest to carry to the conductor in an effort to avoid further difficulties. I have found this a very effective technique in coping with a situation in which language or other problems are anticipated. My own experience suggests that in most places, with the aid of a pocket dictionary, one will be able to find some person who is friendly enough to take the time to work through with you a problem which you have.

The priest and the U.S. couple seemingly were similarly anticipating a similar set of future events, i.e., more confusion getting to the right train. His act of taking them to the gate and providing the note communicate his concern and desire to help.

The ambiguity and the lack of closure will remain high without the aid of an effective interpreter. As noted earlier, the most effective interpreter will be one who has experienced both cultures as well as having facility in both of the languages. The priest, although his exposure to America may have been somewhat limited and not very recent, had some appreciation of the culture of the Americans as well as some facility in American English. It cannot be overemphasized that the knowledge of two languages without a knowledge and understanding of both cultures will result in some very un-satisfactory transactions.

Although there were differences in norms, values, and role expecta-tions, there were some similarities on which the participants could draw. One of these was the shared value for honesty. The establishing of some common reference points is essential for effective communication.

If one were to experience an entire day of transactions of the type re-ported in this chapter, the fatigue level would be quite high and the satisfac-tion level quite low. The time required to deal with even routine requests is greatly increased over that required where homogeneity is higher. Imagine, if you will, the American couple and the travel agent attempting to deal with some abstract issue. It undoubtedly would have been a quite unsatisfactory experience. It would have required even more time and effort; there likely would have been even less certainty as to what meanings were intended and elicited; and they would have lacked the visible, concrete act or product as a check on what outcome had been achieved, beyond mutual frustration. An experience, such as the one reported, also can suggest the great difficulty of attempting to resolve serious social conflicts between or among highly heterogeneous participants. The next two cases are intended to illustrate some of the difficulties and some ways of coping.

EXERCISES

1. If you knew you would be engaging in a transaction at Level 5 of homo-geneity-heterogeneity, what would you do to prepare for the transaction?
2. How would your preparation differ if the transaction were among partici-pants who would be described by:
   a. Set No. 24 (PRI_2 CS_3 KA_2 WV_1)?
   b. Set No. 27 (PRI_2 CS_2 KA_2 WV_2)?
   c. Set No. 26 (PRI_1 CS_3 KA_2 WV_2)?
3. How would your preparation differ from that for set No. 5 (PRI_1 CS_1 KA_1 WV_2) in Level 2 of homogeneity-heterogeneity?

9

The Professor and the Minority Leaders— A Case of Heterogeneity Reducing Predictability

This Level 6 transaction is next to the most heterogeneous classification in the taxonomy. The situation used here to illustrate Level 6 is an intranational one. It's a case of a university professor, who was reared in a middle class U.S. family, working with some leaders in a minority community on a project of interest to the department of which he is a part. He believes that the project will be helpful to the families of the minority group, especially the children.

There is some feeling on the part of the university professor that the members of the minority community have not utilized the advantages available to them. The minority members feel that they have been exploited by the larger society, that there have been lots of promises and nearly always without tangible results.

Many other intranational, as well as international, situations could be used to illustrate this level. Among the intranational ones would be the following two situations:

To begin with is a person who was filing for welfare assistance for the first time. She is from a remote area of the country with limited schooling and with very little contact outside a close-knit neighborhood comprised of others from the area in which she lived before coming to a large industrial city of about a million population. The welfare worker with whom she is talking has always lived in a middle class milieu, has had some college training, and has had limited contact with persons from the very low socio-economic levels.

Next is a poor family with a delinquent child appearing before a judge. The family has always lived in low socioeconomic inner city areas, and has had limited contact with upper middle or upper socioeconomic persons. The judge was born in an upper middle class home and had no contact with lower socioeconomic areas of people prior to becoming a judge.

In the cases cited above, all the parties speak standard American English, although somewhat different versions of it. Each also has his own unique dialect—the university professor with his academese; the judge with his intellectual legal language; the minority group with their community dialect; the poor family and the child with their street dialect; the welfare worker with the governmentese; and the unemployed, unskilled worker with the dialect of her neighborhood. These represent a form of bilingualism which many times is not recognized as such. In the taxonomic description, using only the ends of the continuum, these situations would be listed as sharing a common language. By adding other levels and expanding the categories, further precision of classification could be obtained.

Other situations could be noted, but it is presumed that those mentioned will suggest some of the types of intranational situations, which have all the characteristics of being highly intercultural. As indicated at the beginning of this chapter, the case to be elaborated to illustrate the Level 6 event will be the university professor and his transaction with the minority group, a group with which he has had little prior contact.

THE PARTICIPANTS

The taxonomic description for this case, as shown in Table 4, is as follows:

$$PRI_2 - CS_2 - KA_3 - WV_2$$

There has been a continuing resentment of the majority, of which the professor is a part, by the minority group based on what they perceive as repeated manipulations to exploit them. The minority often feels that the majority has treated them like children, and furthermore, not the way benevolent parents would treat children.

PRI_2 (Perceived relationship and intent):

By the Professor—Here are some people who have not had the advantages which most people in this State have had. I can help them have some of these opportunities. Besides, it will help provide some opportunities for students who need field experience and support some of the university programs. They may very well feel there has been a paternalistic pattern of behavior toward them by all groups who have claimed to want to help. I need somehow to bring them into a program of health improvement. Past efforts have been rejected or ignored and that may very well happen again. They may resent my coming to them with another program.

By the Minority Leaders—Our ancestors were abused by the majority. Now it is more subtle. They make promises of help, but never do anything. They want to study us as though we were some strange thing, and after they study, nothing happens. Some of them can be trusted, but many cannot be trusted. They use us for their purposes. They are arrogant and feel superior. They are not willing to listen to our wisdom.

CS_2 (Code system):

Both the professor and the minority leaders speak fluent standard American English. The professor, of course, has his technical academic language; and the minority members have their own minority dialect which the professor does not know or comprehend. The conversations for the sample transaction set reported here were entirely in standard English, but affected somewhat by the participants' dialects.

KA_3 (Knowledge and acceptance of normative beliefs and overt behaviors):

Normative Beliefs

Of the Professor—Everyone ought to help persons less fortunate than themselves. Decisions should be made democratically. All persons should do everything possible to care for their health. Plan carefully and carry out the plan. Be frugal in the use of resources, your own and those of others. Give children the best care possible. Be prompt and punctual in all you do; never keep others waiting. Share your knowledge with others. Help the poor. Get all the schooling you can and help others to do likewise. Base decisions on the best available data. Work hard. Trust people.

Of the Minority—Be wary of strangers. Rely on natural processes to care for you. One ought not disturb nature. Use only what you need; don't waste resources. Be suspicious of people who want to study you. Watch out for shrewd deals. Children should respect their elders and follow their ways. Enjoy life. Learn about life by living it; the best schooling is living in the world.

The structural level of values is the same for both the professor and the minority, Kohlberg's level two, in which the belief is that rules are necessary for any group to exist and one should adhere to the rules out of concern and respect for all in the group. The values content differs.

For the Professor—The values content includes formal education; health; efficiency; honesty; family; security; cleanliness; orderliness; high standard of living for all; self-help; industriousness; individual initiative; and science.

For the Minority—The values content includes real life experiences; leisure; community; equality; physical prowess; freedom; tradition; self-discipline; and family.

Roles

Some of the roles are the same for the professor and the minority members. They all are spouses and parents, and members of a community. The way they perform those roles differs somewhat. Perhaps a major difference is in the occupational roles.

For the Professor—There are the formal roles of teacher and researcher in the academic environment. This person also is a health clinician, who is certified to provide diagnosis and therapy. He has leadership roles among his academic colleagues.

For the Minority—The occupational roles tend to be hourly workers in a factory or business; some may have their own small business; and some may have supervisory roles in a work force. The particular individuals involved in the transaction reported here have leadership functions within the community, either formal or informal, as they work together to provide for cohesiveness and general well-being of all members of the community.

WV₂ (World view):

NL₂ (Nature of Life)

For the Professor—If you work hard, you'll succeed and have a good life. To have the best life, one delays gratification. Most people can be trusted; we earn trust by the way we behave. There is an order to the universe that man can continue to discover through study and control for his benefit. Death is inevitable so one should prepare for it, but in the meantime, one should use all his knowledge to prolong the physical life.

For the Minority—Life follows natural patterns and one flows with it. Time is endless, so one should not be greatly concerned about time. Life will be good if people are non-violent toward mother earth and toward one another. There is intelligence in all things.

PL₂ (Purpose of Life)

For the Professor—The purpose of life is to: Accumulate resources for one's self and one's family; the more successful a person is the more he accumulates. Use one's knowledge to find improved ways of obtaining and using resources to increase one's own comfort and the comfort of those close to him. Contribute to new knowledge for the present and future generations; this bolsters one's own sense of achievement in providing a "better life" for all.

For the Minority—The purpose of life is to care for one another in their needs and to care for mother earth ... Also to flow with the universal system.

RMC₂ (Relation of Man to the Cosmos)

For the Professor—Man is a superior creature among all life in the universe and has been given control over many aspects of the universe. As man increases his knowledge of the universe, he accumulates increasingly more control over various aspects of the cosmos. There is a recognition of a kind of interdependence among the elements of the cosmos, but man can affect the nature of that interdependence. His concept of a diety is in the Judaic-Christian tradition.

For the Minority—There is a universality of all things. This is represented by the concept of a circle and circles within circles. At one level is the sun, moon, wind, and earth, each different, yet each part of the whole and the whole gets strength and function from each. The concept of the continuing, universal, cyclical pattern of all of life is reproduced in their creations of articles associated with their way of life—living quarters, arrangement of furnishings and art. The pattern also extends to seating arrangements when people assemble. The concept of a diety is one of universal form with no sense of a favored people or need to proselytize for a particular concept of diety. There is a rhythm in all of life and man is part of that rhythm.

THE TRANSACTION

A university professor in the USA has gone to meet with some leaders in a minority community in his state regarding some health programs which might be started. The university professor is from the majority culture in the state and has had very limited contact with the minority group with whom he is meeting.

The meeting initially was arranged by two intermediaries, one from the majority culture who has worked quite a lot with this minority culture, and one from the minority culture who has worked in both the majority and minority cultures. Both intermediaries are highly patient and sensitive persons; and both are committed to more shared activities between the majority and minority cultures. Both are extremely busy and cannot respond to all requests for their help.

The professor has had some coaching by the two intermediaries on some of the differences to expect. He was told to expect a different way of viewing time; and he was reminded that there has been a kind of paternalistic relationship of the majority to the minority over many years; and that there has been a feeling of resentment by the minority regarding the relationship. The professor also was alerted that he would be viewed with suspicion. He was advised to be patient, honest, and to remember that he is a visitor. He also was advised to refer to his conversations with the intermediary from the minority group.

As he arrives, the professor becomes quite aware of some of the differences with which he may have to deal. The meeting time has been set for seven o'clock in the evening. He arrives at the building, a school, a few minutes before seven and no one is there. A little after seven, one or two persons arrive. He introduces himself. They respond, then sit and proceed to talk about their activities of recent days. After about a quarter of an hour he inquires about Mr. A, the person he was supposed to meet, the person who would conduct the meeting.

Each asked the other if they had seen Mr. A and neither had. They continued talking for another 15–20 minutes without either including or excluding the professor, who was feeling more and more uncomfortable. Again the professor inquired as to whether there may have been some mistake about the time of the meeting. Those present didn't think so. After another quarter hour, more or less, the professor asked if there were any way they could contact Mr. A. They said they guessed they could call him. Neither moved to do so immediately. After a few more minutes passed, one of them went outside and called toward a building across on another hill. There was an answer, then after another 30–40 minutes, Mr. A arrived. There was no comment about the time nor about the professor having to wait. (This was about two hours after the professor thought the meeting was to begin).

There was some more visiting among the minority members present (three more had drifted in during the wait), then Mr. A said, "I suppose we should start. What is it that you wanted to talk about?"

PROF: Mr. Y and I had met some weeks ago and he had then talked with you about some opportunities to do some preliminary screening of children for any problems with respiratory diseases. He told me that you would be interested in talking about the possibilities and had told me that we would meet tonight to do that.

MR. A: Yes, he did talk to some of us about that. It sounded like it might be all right. What is it that you want to do?

At this point the professor explains a series of screening tests which will be conducted with members of the minority who are interested. It is pointed out that for the best result, everyone should be tested, but especially the children, so that they may be treated early to prevent serious health problems later. At the conclusion of the presentation, Mr. A speaks.

MR. A: What do you get out of it and what do we get out of it? People from the university always want to study us, but they never do anything about what they find from the study. (There was evident irritation in his voice.)

PROF: We would test the people to detect early symptoms of disease or disorders which could be corrected if properly treated. We would not do the treatment, but would help arrange for the treatment. The survey would offer a field experience for our students who will be doing this kind of work when they leave the university. When students assist with the testing there always will be a regular faculty person supervising the work each student does. Each student must have many hours of this type of intern experience before he graduates and comes to work in your community or some other one.

MR. A: We're not sure whether this is something we would like to have you do. We would like to know more about the tests and what it would mean for our people. We want to believe that you are truly interested in doing something good for us, but we still are not sure.

PROF: If you wish, you could come to our clinic at the university and watch some of the tests, see the equipment which is used, and take some of the tests yourself.

Some of the persons from the meeting agreed to come to the campus. A time was set and the details of the visit were agreed to. When the group came to the campus, some of the same people who attended the first meeting came; others who had not attended the first meeting also came. This required some additional explaining of what was being proposed. This visit gave some further encouragement, but still did not result in an agreement to undertake the screening.

The professor and some of his colleagues again went to the community of the minority. There was further discussion of the procedures, what benefits each might expect, and what followup programs would be carried out.

A mutual goal was eventually set. The professor and his colleagues would do the clinical survey to find the people with problems. They would then try to get help for the people with problems so that they could be treated, and hopefully cured. They felt they had communicated effectively. The survey was conducted and several cases were found which did need attention, some requiring minor surgery. These people were referred to a clinic facility nearby for the followup treatment.

A few weeks later, the professor received a telephone call from the health leader in the community asking when Dr. X would be coming back. He said the Dr. had said, anytime I need help he'll be here. The surgeon had offered to provide his services free, but had pointed out that within the community they would have to arrange for the hospital costs. The health leader then reiterated several times that the professor had said that the university group would provide followup care. It took much effort and repeated attempts to get understanding of the boundaries of followup which the university team could provide. The two intermediaries met with one another, and with the professor; and the intermediary from the minority culture met with the minority leaders. They reviewed what had happened at each meeting and clarified intent and meanings of various statements which were reported.

One outgrowth of the communication between the professor and minority group was a 12-month Federal grant from funds available for the kind of health care required. Further, a coordinator was hired to work within the community to make arrangements for followup care. There continued to be misunderstandings as to what would be done and by whom. At first the intermediaries were called on to help clarify; later the participants generally could resolve the misunderstanding themselves.

ANALYZING THE TRANSACTION

It seems quite apparent that the professor was not prepared for the difference in world view regarding time. He coped with it in the only way he knew; he controlled his frustration and adjusted to the concept of time within the community. He also had a different set of expectations about how meetings are run. Again, the professor adjusted. He was the visitor in this situation.

The impact of the negative perceptions of relationship and intent between the parties is reflected in several ways. One way is the statement: "What do you get out of it and what do we get out of it? University people always survey ... etc." The handling of time also may have been exaggerated by the minority. If they knew the value placed on punctuality by the professor's culture, they may have been more casual than usual in assembling, using this to communicate their irritation with past exchanges they've had with the culture he represents.

It has been established that the participants were at the most heterogeneous level of knowing-accepting (KA_3) normative beliefs and overt behaviors. It seems that the minority group knew but didn't accept the norms, values, and role expectations of the professor; while the professor did not have good knowledge of norms, values, and role expectations; and he would have found that he did not adhere to several of those which were important to the minority.

The caution in agreeing to the survey also indicated a distrust based on prior experiences in their exchanges with the majority culture. Within the three exchanges, some increase in trust of the professor apparently developed. They were willing to go ahead with a plan, which it was later discovered was not understood in the same way by the two groups.

The intermediaries who had arranged the initial contact continued to assist by clarifying the intentions and expectations. They were needed to interpret the messages for the two groups, even though on the surface it seemed the two groups were speaking the same language. Had it not been for the intermediaries, the first meeting of the professor with the minority leaders may not have occurred. He had made previous efforts to get such a meeting, but without success. It appears that further briefings on the minority culture would have been helpful.

That aspect of world view in which the minority believes that the father role is to find the problem and correct it contradicts the majority view of each person does as much as he can for himself in finding and correcting the problem. It seems that this was another of the factors contributing to the confusion regarding followup care.

If there had been less heterogeneity between the two groups, they would have been able to anticipate some of the misunderstandings which occurred. They also would have been able to reach agreement in less time as to what might be done regarding the survey and followup. Without the intermediaries, much more difficulty would have been encountered.

Perhaps the two most significant points illustrated by the case cited here are: (a) the importance of intermediaries who know both cultures; and (b) the difficulty of establishing trust in the highly heterogeneous situation. Both of these were necessary conditions for the transactions to develop to a point where some mutual goals could be realized.

EXERCISES

1. If you had been the professor in this case, what would you have done to improve the efficiency of the transactions?
2. If only the intermediary from the majority culture could have accompanied you in your role as professor, what would you have asked the intermediary to do for you?
3. If only the intermediary from the minority culture could have accompanied you in your role as professor, what would you have asked the intermediary to do in the transactions which occurred?
4. Describe a situation which you believe was equally as heterogeneous as that described in this chapter, but which you believe was—
   a. A more efficient transaction.
   b. A less efficient transaction.
5. What contributed to the difference in efficiency of the transactions described in item No. 4?

10

The Outsider Learns to Cope in a Highly Heterogeneous Setting

The case selected to illustrate the most heterogeneous situation (Level 7) is an international one. It could just as well have been an intranational one, since most nations have enough diversity of ethnic groups to have two or more for whom there are extreme differences in beliefs and language. This kind of pluralism is becoming increasingly visible throughout the world. As national boundaries are changed, this also brings new sets of ethnic groups together within a nation. That diversity is present within the international case being used here.

A newly independent nation is planning an extensive irrigation system. It will encompass areas of the country which include three different tribal groups adjacent to the river which supplies water to the region. With a new national government, these homogeneous groups are now involved in more intense interaction than was ever required under colonial rule.

The specific aspect of the communication event on which we'll focus is the set of transactions between a U.S. technical advisor, six representatives of the three tribal areas (two representatives from each), and an interpreter. The interpreter is provided by the Minister of Agriculture to help the technician and the representatives deal with their language differences.

THE PARTICIPANTS

The taxonomic description of the participants for this case, as shown in Table 4 is as follows:

$$PRI_2 - CS_3 - KA_3 - WV_2$$

The dissimilarity is at the limit on all four variables. The U.S. technician has not been in this country before, nor have the tribal representatives ever worked with a person from the USA before. The briefings prior to their coming together have been primarily on technical aspects of their work. The technician expects the tribal representatives to be "backward" people who do not understand modern technology. The tribal representatives expect the U.S. technician to be another of those persons who believe

116

the way the USA does things is the best for everyone, a person who is not willing to listen to the traditional wisdom of the people who lived in the area for centuries. As in each of the previous illustrations, the sampling of elements within each variable is that set deemed most relevant to the reported transactions; it is not an all inclusive set.

PRI₂ (Perceived relationship and intent):

By the Tribal Representatives—The technician will be arrogant, thinking he has all the answers and will want us to do just what he says. He'll expect us to submit to his directives. He'll want us to do what he wants and we will have difficulty doing what we want in the way we want. He'll feel superior to us and we feel we are just as good as he.

By the Technician—These people haven't had much opportunity to work with modern equipment and methods. They'll probably be defensive when I try to tell them the best way to handle this project. They'll probably think I'm trying to control their lives. If the program is to succeed, I'll have to be firm about the way it has to be done. They won't likely be openly hostile, but they will feel resentment toward me, even though the government has asked me to come. If they only knew, I'd just as soon not be here either, but it's a good deal for awhile; and the pay and allowances are great. That will make it easier to take.

CS₃ (Code system):

None of the tribal representatives speak fluent English. Three speak some English; the others know only a few words of English. The technician speaks only American English. Each of the tribal representatives has his own dialect and each of them understands the dialect of the others. There is no national language. The interpreter speaks fluent British English, knows one of the dialects very well, one somewhat and the third not at all. In this position as interpreter, he can act as an effective gatekeeper in the transactions between the technician and the tribal representatives.

KA₃ (Knowledge and acceptance of normative beliefs and overt behaviors):

The Tribal Representatives Believe: Older people always must be respected; one should not disagree with an elder in the group. Always take care not to disrupt the social relations of the group. Be reverent toward one's ancestors, lest your irreverence cause you harm. Work is to be enjoyed and done as a group; enjoy the social aspect of it; everyone does something, helping according to his ability. Polygamy is allowed. Be honest in all relationships will all people.

The Technician Believes: The person who knows the most about the topic should receive the most respect. To the extent possible, one should do things for himself. Work while you work and play while you play; don't mix the two. Strive for the highest possible productivity from all activities in which one is involved. Be honest in all relationships with all people. Always speak out with what you believe. Dress functionally for the activity and physical comfort. Monogamy is required.

The Tribal Representatives Value: Group cohesiveness; traditional wisdom; family; ancestors; simplicity of life style; cooperation; consensual decision making.

The Technician Values: Individuality; scientific knowledge; industriousness; productivity; modern technology; wealth; competition; hierarchical decision making.

For the tribal representatives, the family related roles are the most important and they expect others to emphasize the family roles. For the technician, the work related roles are the most important, and he expects the tribal representatives to give top priority to the roles that involve getting the project plan developed and implemented. He expects to be received as the visiting consultant whose knowledge is unquestioned. They expect him to perform as a consultant who will transmit information which they may consider, then decide what is appropriate for their situation. He is the researcher-teacher from the most modern nation of the world; they are the political appointees to a project in one of the less technologically developed countries of the world. They see themselves as the decision makers; he sees them as the coordinators of decision implementation.

WV₂ (World view):

For the Tribal Representatives: Life is continuous. The seed from the plant produces new plants which produce seed to produce new plants and on and on. One's ancestors are always near and can influence what happens to one. The earth provides bountifully for those who care for the earth. The past and the present are important; the future will take of itself if one doesn't offend the gods or one's ancestors. Time is associated with events such as planting, harvesting, changes in seasons of the year, etc. Time of day is associated with length of one's shadow. If one does what is right, the families will be large and healthy and the crops and animals will be productive and provide much food.

For the Technician: Life is a complex chemical and physical process of which man is learning more year by year. Many aspects of it can be controlled by man. One's ancestors exert influence on one's behavior only in what they teach the person while they are alive. There is an interdependence among various kinds of life. Life is a challenge in which man attempts to solve the riddles to permit his longer survival and enjoy himself.

For the Tribal Representatives: The basic purpose of life is to stay alive and bring honor to one's ancestors. Everyone lives to share with the group and contribute to the well-being of all in the tribe. There is not a sense of individual acquisitiveness or territoriality; there is a sense of protecting the territory of the group and gathering what is needed for the survival of the tribe. Another purpose is to do those things which please one's ancestors; e.g., pouring libations—an elder at a wedding ceremony pours the first drink upon the ground while calling on the ancestors to bless the occasion.

For the Technician: The purpose of life is to acquire individual possessions and the prestige and recognition which accrues from the accumulation of possessions. There is a strong urgency to discover some new thing as much to achieve the recognition as to improve the life of other people. These are not independent, of course, since a new discovery which helps lots of people brings more recognition. Providing well for one's family so children can get a good education to continue discovering more about the nature of life also is an integral part of the purpose.

The Tribal Representatives Believe: Man is subject to the various aspects of nature and can't really do much about it. He should take special care not to interfere with natural processes. Within this context he does use herbs with seeds at planting time; and he may seek assistance of magic to avoid hail damage to crops; etc. These actions he sees as working with nature.

Man should take only as much game as is needed for food; cut trees only as needed for shelter or fuel, etc. He is not a god that he can change earth, the stars, the sun, or the moon. These follow their pattern always. Unusual things are associated with the gods.

The Technician Believes: Man is the only being with reason in the universe and he can use that reason to learn about, understand, and control the energy and forces within the universe for his own benefit. As he increases his knowledge he can bring more and more of the universe under his control.

THE TRANSACTION

The Minister of Agriculture has studied in other countries and observed the increased food production that is possible with irrigation. He has asked each of the three tribes to send two representatives to plan for an irrigation system in their combined area. It's an area where a stream is large and carries an abundance of water for a portion of the year and is nearly dry during a portion of the year. He believes a dam or series of dams may be used to control the flow of water and have it available for crops throughout the growing season.

He has arranged for a technician, an irrigation specialist, to spend one year in the country studying the possibilities and helping initiate plans. He introduced the technician to the tribal representatives at a brief reception and had them schedule a meeting. A sample of the conversation from that meeting will be used to illustrate the Level 7 communication.

As noted in the description of participants, none of the tribal representatives speaks fluent English so the Minister has provided an interpreter.

The differences in normative beliefs and overt behaviors, and in world view also have been noted. The perceived relationship appears to be one that is somewhat antagonistic.

Each of the persons, including the technician has received instruction from the Minister. Now they are assembled, and they have exchanged greetings (which were rather lengthy by the U.S. technician's standards). They have now begun to talk about the irrigation program. The technician is not aware that the conversation already is dealing with the problem, since all are speaking in their own dialect.

After a few minutes the technician becomes impatient and asks the interpreter, whom we'll call I, how he thinks the group should proceed with the discussion of the topic. I tells him in a somewhat terse tone that they already have been talking about the need for irrigation. The technician, in an impatient tone, says that he thought the need already had been decided and that the task now was to determine whether it was feasible; what data would be needed to make that decision; and if feasible, what methods and design of system would be most efficient.

I reports the technician's question and comments to the representatives, using the dialect he knows well. The representatives agree that the Minister was convinced that irrigation was needed; but they state that not all the people were convinced of the need. They feel that they have had enough food and don't see the purpose in producing more than they need.

As the interpreter translates this, the technician is becoming more frustrated and asks if they cannot understand that if they produce more they could sell it to other parts of their country or even on the world market to get money to buy more things for themselves.

At this point I talks again with the six representatives at some length. While they are talking, the technician impatiently starts writing some notes on a pad. He is sketching some additional details on alternatives based on an airplane flight he made over the region within the past week and other data given to him. The flight and other data provided information on terrain, water flow, etc. One of the alternatives is to build a dam and canals along the river to carry the water from the dam to the fields below. After some time, he again gets the attention of I and states that perhaps they could understand better if they saw some examples of what is involved. He then shows the sketches to I and explains the general aspects of the dam and canal alternative.

I translates the technician's statement and sketches for the representatives. There follows some animated discussion with many hand gestures. The technician is not sure whether the discussion is accepting of the notion presented, whether it is understood, or disliked. He has thought his role was primarily to tell what alternative design would be best and what would be required to build it and get it operating.

Soon *I* turns back to the technician and says that the representatives are quite disturbed by the plan. The canals would cross the many paths now used by people to get from their shelter and fields to the river.

The technician at this point is having difficulty controlling his annoyance. He says that he can't understand why the paths should be any problem. Bridges could be built over the canals at selected spots. Furthermore, the people can now get water from the canals.

I points out that the people have favorite spots by the river where they meet when they go for water. He has to explain that going for water is more than just a task. It's a social event too, and the places selected have certain desired features which are valued for their comfort and for the traditions associated with them. (He confirms his statement with the representatives.)

The technician has difficulty understanding the importance of this and points out that man is essentially living on a space ship (earth) with an increasing population and a food producing potential that is reaching its limits. Every bit of technology is needed to prepare for maximum production levels to prevent starvation in most parts of the world. Surely, having enough food is more important than preserving paths to the river.

I translates this statement to the representatives. They say that yes food is important but so are the pathways. There must be some way of meeting both needs. *I* then resumes his effort to explain the importance of the pathways to the technician.

The representatives also have been getting somewhat impatient, at least the nonverbal cues would suggest it—their shuffling about, looking at the technician and *I* talking, and their own talk and gestures toward *I* and the technician are increasing. One of them finally signals *I* that they want to know what is being talked about.

I now turns to the six, while the technician's impatience continues to rise. Finally the technician decides that he must ask the Minister to take some action to get an agreement for the technician to go ahead with the work on the irrigation design. He suggests to *I* that they go talk to the Minister. *I* tells the representatives of the request. All agree and *I* says that he will arrange for a meeting the next morning. This is acceptable since the pattern for consensual decision making also includes a belief that the door of the official is always open to people with problems.

The meeting with the Minister is opened by *I* explaining in the dialect what has transpired and that the plan for a canal would interfere with the pathways. He also states that not all tribes feel the need for more food at this time. There is need to get agreement on the project. Each person presents his views on the matter; the technician is given an interpretation from time to time. He is also asked for his opinion on some aspects of the issues involved. Again the technician becomes quite impatient with the long discussion, not being accustomed to the consensual approach to decisions.

Eventually it is decided that large concrete pipes could be put under the pathways at points where the canal would need to cross them. There is also agreement that the technician may go ahead, in collaboration with local technicians and design an irrigation system. Approximately once each month the technician is to meet with the tribal representatives to explain the design to them, and how it will affect the countryside and people. Then they will go explain it to the people in their tribes and seek approval for continuation with or without modification, as the case may be. *I* will continue to serve as interpreter.

The technician adjusts somewhat to the style of decision making of those with whom he is working, but he does not feel comfortable with it. He also learns a little of the language and more of the culture and becomes more tolerant of it, although never being able to accept it himself. The representatives continue to have difficulty understanding why the technician is so impatient and gets frustrated so easily. His ways are strange and they will be pleased when the task is finished and he can go home. They and the technician come to respect the honesty and integrity of one another, but neither becomes attracted to the life style of the other.

A design is eventually completed which all can accept and construction is started. The technician stays on to supervise the construction, a decision mutually arrived at by the technician and his hosts.

ANALYZING THE TRANSACTION

Keep in mind that only one person had access to all the dialogue in this communication event. That person was *I*, the interpreter. He was the gate-keeper, and what was transmitted between the technician and the tribal representatives was what he understood and considered important. He could control the transaction.

If you feel that you have somewhat less than a complete report of the transaction, remember that the participants also did not have a complete report. The Minister presumably was able to resolve the differences for two reasons: he has an official position, although that is not as significant as it would be in a nonconsensual society; and he is bicultural with the two groups as well as bilingual.

As in all the other cases presented, there was enough tolerance of one another's differences among the participants for the transaction to continue. If that tolerance were not present, the transaction could be quite short, if it got under way; or there might even be open belligerence.

There was the impasse between the technician and the six representatives. This was resolved by the Minister who was bicultural. It is unlikely that the technician with his strong task and productivity orientation could have endured the time required to achieve consensus, working only with the representatives and the interpreter.

The technician was not prepared to wait for each person to "have his say." It seemed to him like a waste of time to listen to all of the details of what each wanted to say; and, of course, the translation process required much more time, even when the translation was a summary. The technician had difficulty understanding why the "top" person did not merely say what he wanted done, then everyone would get the work started. That was true even though the technician saw himself as committed to democratic processes. The representatives, on the other hand, could not understand how anyone would want to decide on a course of action until all persons had expressed their opinions and questions.

A person in a situation such as that presented here must have a strong tolerance for ambiguity and uncertainty. Not only does he feel on the outside looking in when he does not know the language, he has the added uncertainty from not knowing the world view, values, and other normative beliefs and behaviors of the persons with whom he is attempting to communicate. Although the technician had been briefed about the beliefs and behavior patterns of his hosts, it still was a strong test of his self-control to cope with patterns so different from his own.

For the technician, tradition only gets in the way of progress; and he would work forcefully to prevent tradition delaying a new development. When he faces a high priority placed on preserving traditional pathways, he becomes very frustrated. His drive for action leads to his discussion of the importance of having enough food, and eventually leads to asking for the Minister to intercede. The technician expected the Minister to rather quickly give the decision and was not prepared for the extended discussion to achieve consensus. His expectation of a quick decision and action again added to his annoyance and frustration.

For one accustomed to controlling his environment, the lack of control experienced by not having the language facility of those with whom he is working, and the lack of a thorough understanding of the system, can induce strong feelings of helplessness and frustration. The final arrangements for his work provide periods of control, then he again goes through the consensual decision process in the approval of the designs.

Note two factors which helped to keep the transactions from disintegrating. One factor was the tolerance for difference which each was able to muster; the other was the discovery of the honesty and integrity of each in presenting themselves. The following will illustrate the operation of those two factors.

In spite of his annoyance and impatience, the technician was willing to concede the importance of preserving the pathways; and he was willing to take the time, although somewhat grudgingly, to get the input from local people and to listen to others' views. The representatives also were willing to endure the technician's continual pushing to speed up the decision and action, recognizing, but not accepting for themselves, his different perspective of time. These and other acts indicated tolerance for the differences and helped keep the transactions from breaking down.

As for the honesty-integrity factor, the technician became impressed with the manner in which each person's views were accepted and considered in the decision process. There was no effort to conceal anyone's views, nor to consider them unimportant. The representatives, on the other hand, learned to respect the technician for his candor in stating his beliefs. From the operation of those two factors, a level of trust emerged which permitted the participants to continue their transactions and to complete the task.

To achieve effective communication at this level of heterogeneity, it is essential that there be a bilingual-bicultural intermediary, and a set of good faith assumptions among the participants. With either of these missing, one may expect varying degrees of difficulty, even complete chaos. The good faith assumptions include consideration of the other as a "person," not as an object to be manipulated and moved about without regard to the other's needs and wishes. This base of approaching the transaction comes from a person with a positive feeling toward self, not one who is egotistic, fearful, defensive, or paranoid.

What has been presented is not an exaggerated situation; more extreme and difficult situations could have been presented. The case used here could and has occurred among participants of the same nationality, as well as between nationalities. Hopefully, it illustrates for you some aspects of communication among highly heterogeneous participants.

EXERCISES

1. In what ways, if any, would you have recommended a different approach to the Chapter 10 situation by—
   a. The technician?
   b. The minister?
   c. The intermediary?
   d. The tribal representatives?
2. To what extent do you think it is possible to increase your tolerance for ambiguity and uncertainty? How would you go about increasing—
   a. Your own tolerance?
   b. The tolerance of a person whom you were orienting for a Level 7 situation?
3. What sources would you use in preparing yourself or recommend to another in preparing for a transaction at Level 7 of heterogeneity?
4. Describe persons whom you believe should, if at all possible, avoid transactions at Level 7 of heterogeneity.
5. Describe the type of persons you believe would be most successful in transactions at Level 7.

11

Some Guidelines for
the Intercultural Communicator

Some specific suggestions for communicators will be summarized in this chapter. There will be some suggestions that apply in any situation, as well as those which are most pertinent to intercultural situations.

In keeping with the theme of this book, the first task should be to determine the level of heterogeneity of the participants. That is one aspect of that most famous of communication truisms: formerly stated as "Know your audience", more recently as "Know the participants in the transaction." Some would claim that one cannot do well at "other" analysis until one has mastered self-analysis. Thus, we add: "Know yourself." One technique sometimes used to help us know ourselves is writing 20 statements in answer to the question, "Who am I?" (Kuhn and McPartland, 1954). Other helps for knowing self and others are available in books such as that by Johnson (1972).

It requires some knowledge of the self and other in a transaction to determine the level of heterogeneity. We have assumed thus far that the variables already discussed are the more crucial ones in influencing communication outcomes. Thus those variables offer the framework for getting to know the participants. It still leaves the question as to how one gets that knowledge most efficiently.

GETTING TO KNOW YOU AND ME

Undoubtedly the most effective way of getting to know "others" is to live among them, interacting with them openly and intimately. This is not always possible, even in the long range. Certainly for the first meeting with highly heterogeneous others, it is necessary to use secondary sources. Among these are: (a) mass media—print, television, radio, and film; (b) talking with persons from one's own culture who have been in close interaction with the others; and (c) talking with persons from the other culture who now live in your culture. Persons from one's own culture having a lengthy successful experience in the other culture will likely provide more candid, complete, and accurate advice than will a person from the other culture in a pre-entry briefing. Such a source can be invaluable in facilitating the initial and continuing communication.

What questions should one ask to most quickly and effectively learn what is needed to effectively communicate with others? The questions which follow are not claimed to be the only set or an all-inclusive set. It is believed that they will get well beyond the usual superficial or stereotypic views of the other.

If you are collecting data on the other culture before the intercultural contact, the questions may be more direct. If you are getting information directly from a person within the culture, a person whom you are meeting for the first time, then you adapt to the rules of that culture regarding directness of questioning. The problem is to know before the fact what those rules are.

In either case, some of the important things to learn to aid in your communication are:

1. What must one do to get along?
2. What must one not do?
3. What ought one to do?
4. What ought one not do?
5. What is one allowed to do?
6. What are the sanctions for not following the cultural rules?
7. How do persons in this culture view themselves and the world about them?
8. What verbal and nonverbal codes are most critical to know?
9. How direct and open are people in their communication with one another? How does this differ, if at all, for strangers?

Ideally, you will have a briefing through some of the sources noted earlier so that you have answers in the other culture. If the transaction involves a specific issue or topic, then the position of the other on that topic also is very important information to have.

Given the set of behaviors one must or must not adhere to and the set of allowed behaviors, one may estimate how tolerant persons in the host culture will be. When the range of allowed behaviors is relatively large, then high tolerance for difference would be anticipated. When the range of allowed behavior is very small, one may anticipate relatively high intolerance of differences.

Very often when people first meet, they ask about place of residence, occupation, family, and perhaps places of travel. They usually ask rather superficial questions, questions which are presumed to be very safe, but are not revealing. These questions usually do not give much insight about the other person and do not help much in communicating with that person. The questions listed on the preceding page give more insight as to what is important in influencing the other person's life and communication.

In some settings with some persons, you may use a very direct approach such as: "If I'm to communicate effectively with you, we need to know much more about one another than we do now. Some of the things I'd like to know as a start are _____." In some cultures, the norms will preclude such a direct approach. It may, in some cases, be approached on a general third person basis with the other more in the role of consultant on the culture. In other cases, one may have to go very slowly and accumulate the knowledge by observing; and hope, in the meantime, not to commit social errors which seriously impede future transactions.

If you are getting the information about another culture in general, the questions may be asked in a more direct fashion. If you are in conversation with another person for whom you wish the information, the questions are approached more cautiously and may more appropriately be woven into the context of conversation.

An honesty which expresses uncomfortable feelings in an unknown situation and a desire to learn, often can help establish a rapport which allows you to get needed information to carry on further transactions. It might be expressed as: "I feel very uncomfortable in this situation because I don't know enough to know how I'm expected to behave. Would you be willing to tell me some things I should know so as not to offend people?

Each person has his own style. In using his own style, he probably will perform reasonably well in his information gathering if he is tolerant of others, responds to them as a worthwhile "person," and shows honest feelings of friendliness through the universal nonverbal expressions of happiness and friendliness, and the desire to behave "properly."

YOU AS PERSON

My name is important to me because it encapsules a whole set of beliefs about who I am and what I am. Your name is important to you for the same reason. That's why it's important to me to have my name pronounced correctly; that's why it's important for me to pronounce your name correctly. It also helps to know if there are special meanings attached to your name.

Knowing your name and speaking it properly is one way of responding to you as "person," not in some stereotypic sense, or as some kind of impersonal object. Also involved, in responding to you as "person," is to be sensitive to your feelings, your needs, your capacities, and your sense of belonging. This requires some degree of empathy in our relationship. It helps remove anxiety, fear, and feelings of threat in the relationship. It opens the way for effective communication.

A common way of referring to empathy is the capacity to put yourself in the "other's shoes," i.e., to look at the world the way the other person does. One definition of empathy I have found quite useful is a two-sided one. It involves projecting myself into the position of the other and saying, "If I were there, this is how I would think, feel, and act." The other aspect of empathy is to know more about you and about the event you are experiencing; and knowing you, I would mentally role play how you would feel, think, and act in the situation in which I find you. If I know little about you, I'm forced to operate from the projection side; as I learn more about you, I can operate more from the role-taking side.

A person who has experienced the death of a loved one can empathize with another who is now experiencing the loss of a loved one. A person who has been stranded in a strange culture without the knowledge of the language can empathize with a newcomer who is experiencing the same dilemma in one's own culture. One who has been an interpreter can empathize with a person attempting to interpret for two groups who do not share a common language or beliefs. A teacher who has failed a course in school, after working very hard, can empathize with a student in that situation. On the other hand, a teacher who never had any difficulty in passing a course will probably not be able to empathize with the student who is having difficulty passing a course.

The situations just cited illustrate the importance of having had an experience in order to appreciate how another feels in that situation. If I've been in a similar situation to one you are experiencing, I'll assume that I can empathize with you, i.e., "feel as you feel." As I learn more about you, I may discover some ways in which you respond differently than I do. You may attach different meanings and significance to such things as death, failure, success, birth, etc. Until I know how you view those events, I'll have difficulty empathizing with you.

From a communication perspective, to be empathic requires a special sensitivity to all available cues in the situation. It is this sensitivity to cues, and enough knowledge of you to take your role as you would play it, that contributes to my having empathy with you. If you also can take my role in the situation, we have an empathic relationship. Sensitivity to cues and the ability to take the other's role are great assets in any transaction.[1]

As the heterogeneity of participants increases, the possibility of accurately taking the role of the other declines. However, the sensitivity to cues, if well developed, is still a valuable asset. Thorough briefing about the other as a person will assist in the role taking.

Children within homogeneous groups imitate others, then eventually generalize the behaviors they observe. They play at being mother and father; teacher and student; storekeeper and customer; etc. Through this process of imitating and generalized role playing, they internalize the role expectations for their group.

[1]The teacher in the Level 4 case, Chapter 7, demonstrated this.

For the outsider preparing to enter a situation requiring transactions with heterogeneous others, role playing is an effective way to learn the role expectations. This may be arranged with someone of my own culture who has been in sufficient contact with the other culture to become well acculturated; or it may be with someone from the other culture who is available within my own culture. Reading drama, which realistically portrays various roles within the other culture, offers a vicarious role playing experience which will help prepare for entry into that culture.

The role playing permits me to get to know you as a generalized member of your culture. However, I still must have the contact with you to get to know the unique person you are. It requires the level of trust which allows us to share aspirations; beliefs about what is true, important, right, and good; and our feelings about various aspects of our world. At this point, we can engage in transactions with each other as "persons"; we can move toward empathic transactions.

WE NEED FEEDBACK

An Australian friend told me that it came as a great shock to him to find after two or three weeks that words he had been using did not have a shared meaning between him and those with whom he had been communicating. This illustrates the need to give and seek feedback.

Feedback is, I believe, one of the most important elements in the communication process. It is the part of the process which provides a self-correcting function within the process. It's the message or set of messages which identifies lack of shared meanings and the subsequent message or messages used to determine that shared meanings have been achieved.

When some overt act is called for in the communication, the performance or nonperformance of that act provides a positive check on the extent to which the meanings have been shared. One can see whether the anticipated act actually was performed. When an immediate overt act is not involved, some means of obtaining feedback should be planned. One of the difficulties is to do this, either intraculturally or interculturally, in a way that is not offensive.

In either situation, it generally is helpful if I, as the one desiring feedback, take the initiative in offering it as a check of my reception of the message. It may take the form: "Let me see if I understood correctly. What I understand from what you said is _____. What did I omit or change?" Asking for it from the other person may take the form: "Let me check to see if our understanding is the same. What is that you now expect me to do and what do you believe that I expect you to do?" Or one might say: "If I'm understanding correctly, you believe _____." A paraphrasing of the other's statement offers another set of words as a meaning check.

A person in a homogeneous setting not accustomed to using feedback checks may be more likely to be offended than is someone in a situation recognized by both participants to be heterogeneous. There is more likely to be an expectation of needing to check for error in the heterogeneous situation. In either case, I believe that candor can be useful, a candor which states that I am a firm believer in feedback as a check on the meanings we share: "I hope you'll understand that when I ask for feedback I'm wanting to be sure I'm interpreting what you say as you intended."

The universal nature of facial expressions to show emotion has been noted. Recognizing that persons from different cultures, and even within cultures, differ in the extent to which they show emotion, these facial expressions may still effectively signal difficulties. There may be a surprised or puzzled look; or some nonverbal cue of an emotion that seems incongruous with the response you intended. This is the time to say that you feel that you may not have communicated what you thought or intended.

One of the cautions from international students is to be prepared for the possibility that someone may answer a question without knowing the answer because they do not want to be in the position of not knowing. In somewhat the same context is the "polite yes"[2] which may be given more often in the intercultural setting where the person wishes to be very careful not to offend.

For the first dilemma, one safeguard is to seek the same information from more than one source. At least this will provide a reliability check if no check of accuracy is available. If there is a discrepancy between the two sources, it's time to seek another source. If the third one is different from the other two, ... well, better luck tomorrow.

The second dilemma, the "polite yes," may be avoided, to some extent, at least, by providing alternatives which require choices rather than asking questions of the yes-no variety. Also, remember that questions which ask what, where, when, who, why, or how cannot be answered yes or no. Thus, the questioning style may minimize the danger. The 5-W's and the H questions are better for feedback than those questions which can be answered yes or no. When asked, "Do you understand?" it often is embarrassing to say no. It's better to ask, "What did you understand?"

One of the more obvious times when one would ask for feedback is when there appears to be a contradiction between verbal and nonverbal cues. To say, "I feel I'm probably misunderstanding something," may be a useful way of seeking clarification where the uncertainty is high. It's an invitation for the other to help me out of my difficulty. It does not come then so much like an accusation of the other.

In seeking and giving feedback, I believe it is essential not to threaten the ego of the other. Only in this way can I gain the benefit to be derived from feedback.

[2]In some cultures, one does not say "no" to a stranger.

YOUR HELPFUL INTERMEDIARY

In some cultures, intermediaries are often used even among homogeneous others as a way of minimizing conflict and "saving face." This third party can presumably serve as an interpreter to clarify messages and repair communication breakdowns. This person presumably can synthesize the points of view of the parties involved and establish the basis for shared meaning and agreement.

It has been stated previously that intermediaries become increasingly necessary as the interculturalness of the participants increases. Two questions are important in this context—what kind of intermediary should one select; and what is the optimum way of using the intermediary?

It is quite obvious that when participants in a transaction do not share a common code system, they must have someone who can translate between the two or more languages for them. It was noted earlier in this book that language is intertwined with culture. This requires that one know the culture in order to have the full capability of understanding and using the language of that culture. Thus, if one is to have an effective intermediary, that intermediary must be bicultural, or multicultural, as the case may require.

It is highly desirable to agree with the intermediary that he discuss with the participants their intent in various statements. This is especially important in handling idioms, metaphor, and other figurative language. I would feel much more comfortable with the intermediary who indicates some problem with translating a figure of speech. One solution to these situations is to explore together some alternative phrasings and agree on which is most likely to elicit the subtleties of meaning desired.

As noted in the earlier discussions of code systems, there are different interpretations of verbal and nonverbal symbols, even among those who presumably speak the same language. The intermediary who has a good understanding of the concept of relativity of meaning can be much more effective than one who lacks that understanding. He will take the lead in the kind of discussion mentioned in the preceding paragraph. He will be aware of the notion that one's language has some influence on the way that person structures his reality, and he will strive to communicate the intent of the participants rather than word-for-word translations. That, however, can introduce the risk of the intermediary misinterpreting the intent. To minimize that risk, the intermediary should make extensive use of feedback.

If one can afford the luxury of two intermediaries, then one ideally would have culture A as his primary culture and would also have lived and actively participated in culture B. The other intermediary would have culture B as his primary culture and would have lived and actively participated in culture A. Where there were questions of interpretation, these two intermediaries should then be in a better position to achieve valid consensual meanings than would participants operating with one intermediary.

Another characteristic of the intermediaries should be their tolerance for difference, ambiguity and other factors which might induce stress and tension. Particularly in the highly intercultural situation, impatience and tension are likely to develop with the delays required to achieve shared meanings. If the intermediaries cannot tolerate this kind of tension, their effectiveness will decline.

The intermediaries also should have an intense commitment to achieve high fidelity communication. In this connection, they need to understand the importance of achieving a positive working relationship among participants in order to get shared meanings at the content level of the transaction. They should have an understanding of the operation of selective perception and relativity of meaning. That knowledge can help them be more alert to possible misinterpretations. They also should understand and appreciate the concept of feedback as an important aspect of communication.

To get the optimum benefit in working with intermediaries, participants in a transaction should get from the intermediary crucial knowledge of the other prior to the start of the transaction. The participants can discuss with the intermediaries what they expect to be the critical aspects of the transaction. If both have had an opportunity to do this prior to the start of the transaction, there will be fewer surprises for the intermediaries, and they can perform their translating, synthesizing, mediating functions more effectively.

During the transaction, the participants who share with the intermediary[3] their feelings of uncertainty, anxiety, frustration, etc., can expect the intermediary to handle the transaction more effectively. He can help control the rate of the transaction, either by slowing it down or speeding it up; he can probe for more or less detail; he can bring in helpful metaphors to establish common reference points, etc. Developing good rapport with the interpreter is essential to effective communication.

The intermediary who is interested in the people with whom he is working, and who wants to help them satisfy their needs, will contribute much to a satisfying and fruitful transaction for the participants.

"IF I MAY ASSUME ..."

One of the difficulties for all of us in most situations is to suspend judgment until we check our assumptions. Again, as the interculturalness of the situation increases, the number of unconfirmed assumptions tends to increase. As noted earlier, the assumptions we make are based on our beliefs about our world. As the beliefs of the participants increase in diversity, the difference in assumptions will increase.

Part of the solution to handling our assumptions is to increase the data we have on the other participants and the situation. It also is desirable to

[3]See Chapter 8 for an example.

check assumptions with the other participants. The most direct way is to state the assumptions from which we are operating. By doing so, we can learn whether these are the same assumptions the other person is using; or whether the other has data which either support or refute our assumptions.

We can not avoid assumptions in what we say and what we do. However, there is no reason for us to be unaware of the assumptions from which we are operating. In all communication, the most dangerous assumption and the one most often made is that the words and other symbols which I use have the same meaning for you that they have for me. Our frequent use of feedback will help us check that assumption.

Periodic use of critical inference tests of the type developed by Haney (1967) and others can be very helpful in establishing the habit of checking our assumptions and suspending judgment until we have done so.

RULES FOR TRANSACTIONS

Persons from other cultures have told me that they experienced high uncertainty about how to start, how to interrupt and how to terminate a transaction. I, too, have experienced that uncertainty.

Perhaps the most common way of *initiating* transactions is to comment to the other about something both of you are experiencing. This may explain why weather is so often used as a conversation starter. The start may be some reaction to an event occurring within sight or sound of both of you; it may be your feeling about the event.

Another kind of topic for starting a transaction may be some one of the human universals noted in Chapter 1. I've observed that people often use place of residence, occupation, some world event, or some item about family as a topic for starting conversations. It may be that the basic message in all of these is not what appears on the surface, but a message that I would like to talk with you.

Interrupting within the transaction to take a turn at speaking or to shift topics is even more difficult for many persons. The person from another culture is as unsure of the rules here as they are in many other aspects of the transaction. Children are often told not to interrupt while others are talking, thus a pattern of turn taking becomes established. But, how does one know when the other is finished talking?

As we grow older within our own culture we become attuned to the cues, however subtle they may be, for the appropriate time to interrupt. It may be a slight pause in speech; it may be a nonverbal tilt of the head or other gesture; and there are times when a person will, in eagerness, cut in when another has not finished. Sometimes in the USA, the other will say, "Please let me finish," or "There's one more thing I wanted to say," or some similar statement. Often we are not aware of these cues until some "outsider" asks about them; even then we may not be aware enough to answer.

In some cultures where there is a strong hierarchical relationship among participants, the superior may invite the subordinate to speak. The subordinate knows that he must await that invitation. The cue in that situation is more easily recognized than in a more equalitarian setting.

Continuation of the transaction also has several variations. It may proceed at differing rates. It may be very expository, or metaphorical. It may be meandering, or very direct and pointed; very terse, or very elaborated. The rules in this regard vary from culture to culture; and may vary from situation to situation. The pattern of the transaction is one of the things that a person going to another culture should learn about prior to going, to the extent possible. As with most human behaviors, practice is helpful.

Continuation of a transaction requires the stages of "openings" covered in Chapter 1. For a transaction to continue, there must be mutual responsiveness, congruent functional identities, and a shared focus. Knowing the rules of transactions within the culture helps to accomplish the four stages of openings smoothly and in a mutually satisfying way.

Persons with the U.S. middle class business orientation may alienate a person from another culture by going too quickly to the topic which they wish to discuss. In some cultures, people talk about many things before coming to the topic on which a decision is sought. Lack of knowledge of these rules can seriously interfere with the effectiveness of the transaction.

Termination of the transaction may be a problem, too. You may have heard someone say, "That person doesn't know how to stop talking."

Here again participants may have difficulty with knowledge of the very subtle cues that are part of some cultures. In the U.S. bureaucratic culture, the superior may stand up or ask if there are other items to discuss, to signal an end to the transaction. If the other is aware of the cue, this will likely terminate the transaction.

Another pattern often used is for one of the participants to state some next commitment that requires terminating the transaction. Sometimes this is a vague statement initiated by looking at a clock and saying, "I didn't realize how late it is; I must go." In some social situations, serving refreshments may be the signal that the host or hostess wishes to conclude the occasion.

Whatever the setting, often participants will make some comment about seeing one another again, comparable to the USA, "See you later." It is used when there already is an agreement as to time and place for a continuation; or it may be used when there is little probability of seeing the person again. It may be that it's a statement of reluctance to terminate the transaction, a wish that it could continue or be repeated; in a way it expresses satisfaction with the transaction. It also may be an habitual polite response, a feeling of need for some terminating statement.

There also may be rules as to *time and place* to discuss certain topics. Under the discussion of taboos some examples were given of topics which were not to be discussed at some times and places. There also are rules about what is the best time and place to discuss certain topics. Again, one should be alert to these and learn them for the culture in which one will engage in transactions.

INFINITELY ALIKE—INFINITELY DIFFERENT

One of the philosophical arguments regarding social science qualifying as a science deals with the uniqueness of humans in contrast to other aspects of the universe. One point of view holds that an entity within the universe is on one hand very similar to all other entities of that type; on the other hand it is very different from all the other entities of that type. All rocks, e.g., have many common characteristics; yet the structure of each rock is in some way unique. So it is with humans, too.

In our relationship with other humans we may choose to focus on the similarities or we may choose to focus on the differences. For effective communication, it seems essential that we balance our focus to take into account both the similarities and the differences.[4] We need to establish some commonalities before we can achieve shared meanings which are necessary for us to carry on transactions. At the same time we must be aware of the differences and take them into account to minimize the extent to which the differences may prevent achieving shared meanings.

The main contention of this document has been that as heterogeneity increases, the difficulty of achieving shared meanings increases, making communication more difficult and with less predictable outcomes. Identifying the level and nature of that heterogeneity will facilitate coping with it so as to achieve more efficient communication.

SOME UNANSWERED QUESTIONS

Thus far, attention has been mainly on the application of the homogeneity-heterogeneity notions in transactions. There are several unanswered questions as to how the variables used in the taxonomy affect communication outcomes. Among those questions which still need attention to improve our communication are the following:

1. What is the threshold level of heterogeneity of participants beyond which transactions between those participants cannot occur?
2. Which of the variables exerts the greatest impact on the efficiency of communication?
3. For which combinations of variables is heterogeneity most detrimental to or facilitative of efficient communication?

[4]The cases in Chapters 5–10 offer illustrations of attending to similarities and differences.

4. To what extent is the effect of level of heterogeneity generalizable across all social situations and all topics; and to what extent is it topic and situation specific?
5. To what extent is it necessary to reduce heterogeneity among participants before they can communicate effectively?
6. What measures of effectiveness and efficiency are needed before it is possible to satisfactorily answer the preceding questions?

Obviously, this is not a complete set of questions; it's merely a suggestive set of those which may be generated from the taxonomic base to guide further study.

EXERCISES

1. Describe a situation in which you believe you made good use of feedback.
2. Describe a situation in which you used feedback poorly. What could you have done to improve your use of feedback?
3. Identify a person in another culture with whom you would like to communicate effectively. Describe a role playing activity you would use to prepare for that transaction.
4. What information would you need in order to conduct meaningful role playing for the situation you described in exercise #3? How would you obtain that information?
5. What characteristics do you possess that you think would contribute to your success in highly intercultural communication situations? Which of your characteristics would interfere with your success in such a situation?

Bibliography

Althen, Gary L. and Jaime, Josephine. "Assumptions and Values in Philippine, American, and Other Cultures," in *Readings in Intercultural Communication*, Vol. 1, Regional Council for International Education, University of Pittsburgh, Pa. 15213, 1971.

Blau, Peter M. and Scott, W. Richard. *Formal Organizations*. Chandler Publishing Co., 1962.

Blubaugh, Jon A. and Pennington, Dorothy L. *Crossing Difference: Interracial Communication*, Charles E. Merrill Publishing Co., Columbus, Ohio, 1976.

Brown-Parker, John. *The Design, Development, and Field Testing of A Technique To Measure The Effectiveness of Adult Education Instructors Managing Their Verbal Communication of Intent When Establishing the Instructor/Learner Relationship*, Mich. State Univ. Diss. East Lansing, MI, 1982.

Bryan, G., Darrow K., Morrow, D., and Palmquist, B. *Transcultural Study Guide*, Volunteers in Asia, Box 4543, Stanford, Calif. 94305, 1975.

Bunker, Robert M. and Adair, John. *The First Look At Strangers*. Rutgers University Press, New Brunswick, N.J., 1959.

Condon, John C. and Yousef, Fathi. *An Introduction to Intercultural Communication*, Bobbs Merrill, Indianapolis, Ind., 1975.

Couch, Carl and Hintz, Robert A. *Constructing Social Life*, Stypes Publishers, 12 Chester St. Champaign, Ill., 1975.

Darnell, Donald and Brockriede, Wayne. *Persons Communicating*, Prentice-Hall, Inc., Englewood Cliffs, N.J., 1976.

Dunn, Lynn P. *American Indians—A Study Guide and Source Book*, R and E Research Associates, 4843 Mission St., San Francisco, Calif. 95070, 1975.

138

Dunn, Lynn P. *Asian Americans—A Study Guide and Source Book*, R and E Research Associates, 4843 Mission St., San Francisco, Calif. 95070, 1975.

Dunn, Lynn P. *Black Americans—A Study Guide and Source Book*, R and E Research Associates, 4843 Mission St., San Francisco, Calif. 95070, 1975.

Dunn, Lynn P. *Chicanos—A Study Guide and Source Book*, R and E Research Associates, 4843 Mission St., San Francisco, Calif. 95070, 1975.

Each Guide contains an extensive bibliography and covers three broad areas: identity, conflict, and nationalism vs. integration.

Flavier, Juan. *Doctor to the Barrios*, New Day Publishers, Quezon City, The Phillippines, 1970.
A delightful report of a physician who tells how he established rapport with villagers, and what he learned from them. It contains many examples of effective communication. It records high levels of interculturalness within a nation.

Fuchs, Lawrence H. "Inside Other Cultures," *Peace Corps Volunteer*, 6, June, 1968.

Gantz, Walter. "The Movement of Taboos: A Message Oriented Approach," unpublished paper, 1975, Michigan State University.

Gudykunst, W. B. and Kim, Y. Y. *Communicating With Strangers: An Approach To Intercultural Communication*. Addison-Wesley, Reading, MA, 1984.

Hall, Edward. *Silent Language*, Fawcett, New York, N.Y., 1959.

Haney, William. *Communication and Organizational Behavior—Text and Cases*, Richard D. Irwin Co., Homewood, Ill., 1967.

Harms, L. S. *Intercultural Communication*, Harper & Row, New York, N.Y., 1973.

Hunt, Chester L. and Walker, Lewis. *Ethnic Dynamics—Patterns of Intergroup Relations in Various Societies*, The Dorsey Press, Homewood, Ill. 60430, 1974.

Johnson, David. *Reaching Out*, Prentice-Hall, Englewood Cliffs, N.J., 1972.

Joyce, Richard. E. *Relationships Between Information About and Attitudes Toward Other Nations—A Propositional Inventory*, Ph.D. Diss., Michigan State University, 1973.

Kuhn, Manford H. and McPartland, Thomas S. "An Empirical Investigation of Self Attitudes," *American Sociological Review,* 19:1:68–76, 1954.

Layden, Milton. "Hostility, A Big Expense You Can Avoid," *Nation's Business,* Sept., 1970.

Linton, Ralph. *The Tree of Culture,* Alfred A. Knopf, New York, N.Y., 1959.

Mead, George Herbert. *Mind, Self, and Society,* University of Chicago Press, Chicago, Ill., 1934.

Nance, John. *The Gentle Tasaday,* Harcourt Brace Jovanovich, 757 Third Ave., New York, N.Y. 10017, 1975.

Peters, William. *A Class Divided,* Doubleday, Garden City, N.Y., 1971.

Prosser, Michael H. *Intercommunication Among Nations and Peoples,* Harper & Row, New York, N.Y., 1973.

Redfield, Robert. *Folk Culture of Yucatan,* University of Chicago Press, Chicago, Ill., 1941.

Rich, Andrea L. *Interracial Communication,* Harper & Row, New York, N.Y., 1974.

Richmond, P.G. *An Introduction to Piaget,* Basic Books, Inc., New York, N.Y., 1970.

Roe, Robert; Lumanta, Melinda; and Sarbaugh, Lawrence. "A Taxonomic Approach To World View As A Sensitizing Concept In The Process of Intercultural Communication: Comparison of Two Data Sets." *The Michigan Association of Speech Communication Journal* 20:1:1–14, 1985.

Rokeach, Milton. *The Nature of Human Values.* The Free Press, New York, N.Y., 1973.

Ruben, Brent D. and Budd, Richard W. *Human Communication Handbook—Simulations and Games,* Vol. 1, Hayden Book Company, Inc., Rochelle Park, N.J., 1975.

Samovar, Larry A. and Porter, Richard E. *Intercultural Communication—A Reader,* Wadsworth Publishing Co., Inc., Belmont, Calif., 1972, revised 1976.

Sarbaugh, Lawrence E. *Generality of the Dimensions of Source Evaluation Across Language/Cultural Systems,* Ph.D. Diss., Michigan State University, 1967.

Sitaram, K. S. and Cogdell, Roy T. *Foundations of Intercultural Communication*, Charles E. Merrill Publishing Co., Columbus, Ohio, 1976.

Smith, Alfred G. *Communication and Culture*, Holt, Rinehart & Winston, Inc., New York, N.Y., 1966.

Smith, M. Brewster. *Social Psychology and Human Values*. Aldine Publishing Co., Chicago, Ill., 1969.

Useem, Ruth and Downie, R. D. "Third Culture Kids," *Today's Education*, Journal of NEA, Sept.–Oct. 1976.

UNESCO—*Getting the Message Across*, The UNESCO Press, The United Nations, New York, N.Y., 1975.

Watzlawick, P., Beavin, J., and Jackson, D. *Pragmatics of Human Communication*, Norton, New York, N.Y., 1967.

Wenberg, John and Wilmot, W. *The Personal Communication Process*, John Wiley & Sons, New York, N.Y., 1973.

Whorf, Benjamin. *Language, Thought and Reality*, John Wiley & Sons, New York, N.Y., and MIT Press, Cambridge, Mass., 1956.

Appendix A:

Shorthand Symbols

Used in Taxonomy

1. *Code Systems:*
   CS_1—code system is the same for both (or all) participants
   CS_2—In addition to both (or all) participants having a common code system, one set of the participants has a second code system which is not shared
   CS_3—code system is different for both (or all) participants
2. *Intent Dimensions:*
   I_1—sharing and helping intent
   I_2—ignoring intent
   I_3—disrupting, dominating, injuring intent
3. *Knowing-Accepting of Normative Patterns of Beliefs and Overt Behaviors:*
   KA —know and accept normative beliefs and behaviors of the other
   $\overline{K}$A —don't know but have similar normative beliefs and behaviors as other
   K$\overline{A}$ —know the normative beliefs and behaviors of the other but don't accept them
   $\overline{KA}$ —don't know and could not accept, even if known, the normative beliefs and behaviors of the other
   KA_1—three most homogeneous categories* of knowing-accepting of normative beliefs and behaviors among the participants
   KA_2—three intermediate categories* of knowing-accepting of normative beliefs and behaviors among participants
   KA_3—four most heterogeneous categories* of knowing-accepting of normative beliefs and behaviors among participants
4. *Perceived Relationship Dimensions:*
   F_1 —positive end of continuum of feelings toward one another
   F_2 —negative end of continuum of feelings toward one another

*See complete set in Table 4 on page 57 .

G_1—goals of participants are compatible and mutually shared

G_2—goals of participants are incompatible and conflicting

H_1—participants perceive themselves in an equal (non-hierarchical) position in relation to the other

H_2—participants perceive themselves in highly hierarchical, superior-subordinate position in relation to the other

5. *Perceived Relationship—Intent Continuum:*

PRI₁ -homogeneous end of the perceived relationship and intent continuum; it represents the combination $F_1G_1H_1I_1$

PRI_2—heterogeneous end of perceived relationship and intent continuum; it represents the combination $F_2G_2H_2I_3$

6. *World View Continuum:*

WV_1—participants have similar world views

WV_2—participants have different world views

7. *World View Dimensions:*

NL —nature of life

PL —purpose of life

RMC—relation of man to cosmos

Appendix B:

Glossary

1. *Accepting*—The belief in, and overt behavioral adherence to, the normative patterns of the society.
2. *Attitudes*—That set of beliefs which pertain to one's liking or not liking of an object which leads to a predisposition to act in regards to that object.
3. *Beliefs*—All of the things, single or in sets, which a person at a given time accepts as true of the world he lives in, including the relationship between and among entities.
4. *Code system*—The combination of verbal and nonverbal utterances and acts which may be expected to elicit similar meanings in oneself and homogeneous others.
5. *Channel, direct*—Those channels of communication in which there is no intervening mechanism or person between the participants in the communication being considered.
6. *Channel, interposed*—Those channels of communication in which there is an intervening mechanism or person between the participants. It may be any of the electronic or print media, or a person who carries messages between two or more other persons.
7. *Communication*—The process of using signs and symbols which elicit meanings in another person or persons. It has occurred when at least one person has assigned meaning to a verbal or nonverbal act of another.
8. *Culture*—It is composed of psychological, sociological, and technological aspects—beliefs, patterns of behavior, ways of organizing life, tools and artifacts. It is all one inherits from one's ancestors and acquires from those with whom one is in regular communication. (See the Introduction.)
9. *Intent*—What is the outcome the other wants from this transaction and how does he want it to affect me?
10. *Intercultural*—Those activities between or among heterogeneous humans.
11. *International*—Those activities between or among persons from different national states; and those official actions by the representatives of federal governments in the name of a collective action by those nations.
12. *Intracultural*—Those activities between or among homogeneous humans.

143

13. *Knowing*—Knowledge a participant has of the normative patterns of beliefs and overt behaviors of other participants in a transaction.

14. *Norms*—The standard against which one is expected to judge his own behavior and that of others in a society. They encompass what is proper belief and proper behavior.

15. *Openings*—The process of humans moving from a state of independence to interdependent activity. (See page 7.)

16. *Perceived relationship*—Based on cues in the present situation and prior knowledge, the perception of how positively or negatively the other participant(s) in a transaction will respond to me. It is based on three dimensions of perception of other: feelings; goals; and hierarchalness of position and related behavior.

17. *Role expectations*—The anticipated way for another to perform in a given situation; the behaviors associated with the position the other occupies within the social system.

18. *Tasaday*—An isolated tribe discovered in 1971 in the Philippine rain forest region. It is believed this was the first contact they had had with 20th century man.

19. *Taxonomy*—In the realm of plants and animals it is a classification according to natural relationships and the laws and principles of such relationships. In the present context, it is a systematic classification of communication events by levels of homogeneity-heterogeneity of participants.

20. *Transaction*—The process in which two or more persons are mutually involved in delivering and receiving messages via whatever codes are available to them. The emphasis is on the mutuality of behaving simultaneously and sequentially in a way in which the behavior of each influences the behavior of the other. As used in this manuscript, it extends from the establishing of contact to the termination of that contact.

21. *Transactions, complementary*—Transactions are referred to as complementary when there is a superior-subordinate relationship among the participants.

22. *Transactions, symmetrical*—Transactions are referred to as symmetrical when they take place between equals, without either attempting to be in a one-up or one-down position in relation to the other.

23. *Values*—That set of beliefs which pertain to what is important or unimportant, good-bad, or right-wrong. One may speak both of the content and structure of values. The structure concerns the nature of the sanctions for adherence or nonadherence to the values of a culture—externally or internally imposed; external reward-punishment vs some universal principle of justice and fairness. Content refers to a specific value, such as honesty, freedom, wisdom, wealth, etc.

24. *World View*—That set of beliefs about the nature of life, purpose of life, and man's relation to the cosmos. It will include beliefs about science, religion, causality, truth, the natural, supernatural, etc.

Appendix C:
World View Patterns

Mark the items as follows to indicate how well each describes your beliefs about the nature of life, the purpose of life, or the relation of humans to the cosmos.

1. most descriptive
2. fairly descriptive
3. so-so
4. not very descriptive
5. not at all descriptive

1. Questionnaire identification
2. Questionnaire identification
3. Questionnaire identification
4. The purpose of life is to accept self.
5. The purpose of life is to serve others.
6. Life for me is to experience . . . To be.
7. To live is to learn and grow.
8. Life is making mistakes and forgiving other people's mistakes
9. I'm in partnership with the cosmos.
10. The purpose of life is to shape the physical environment for my comfort.
11. Life is to find meaningful relationships.
12. To keep on trying is my guiding purpose.
13. To enjoy each day is a continuing purpose.
14. Life for me is to have goals and reach them.
15. To win is the purpose of living.
16. The purpose of life is to work toward perfection—to be perfect.
17. To live is to get all you can, however you can.
18. My purpose is to control people.
19. Life is to satisfy my needs.
20. Fame is a very worthwhile goal in life.
21. To accumulate all the wealth you can is what one lives for.
22. Human beings are a part of the entire evolution of the cosmos.
23. To live is to be fulfilled: live, breath, see, smile, enjoy.
24. Life is learning how to accept different opinions and ways of thinking.
25. We are part of "it" and therefore the "same" as the cosmos.
26. I'm part of the cosmos (on the nonphysical basis).
27. I'm smaller than the cosmos, yet much bigger than the cosmos.
28. I'm part of a whole; a user, not an abuser, of resources around me.
29. Life for me is to work toward existing in a pleasant manner.
30. A human being is a small cosmos, a perfect force.

31. Being human is an existence seeking closeness to the perfect force.
32. Life offers opportunity for all kinds of experiences.
33. Life for me is to find what I enjoy.
34. Life is learning to survive: physically, socially, mentally, and spiritually.
35. The nature of life is to exist in harmony with nature and other human beings.
36. The purpose of life is to meet our needs without interfering with others' capacity to meet their needs.

Caution: This set of items has had limited testing and should be tested further. Work with it also has been mainly in university communities; work in communities of differing social–economic levels is needed.

Note: This set of items when used with individuals or in group discussions has been very useful in stimulating self reflection on life goals and activities. Those responding to the items have said it was very helpful.

Index

147